SPRINGFIELD MEMORIES

Volume II: The 1940s, '50s & '60s

THE STATE
Journal Register
KEEP YOURSELF CONNECTED.
SJ-R.COM

Copyright© 2010 • ISBN: 978-1-59725-262-1
All rights reserved. No part of this book may be reproduced, stored in a retrieval system or transmitted in any form or by any means, electronic, mechanical, photocopying, recording or otherwise, without prior written permission of the copyright owner or the publisher.
Published by Pediment Publishing, a division of The Pediment Group, Inc. www.pediment.com Printed in Canada

Foreword

If the first volume of *Springfield Memories* depicted the many facets of diverse peoples working to fulfill their dreams, Book Two reflects the fruits of those efforts. In this edition, covering the years from the 1940s through the 1960s, much will be recognized or recalled. Stores and industries with familiar names and purposes are pictured in contrast to the often unknown or long forgotten world of the earlier edition.

Many buildings and businesses pictured are familiar to us today, though perhaps in another form. In many instances, these pictures bring back memories of places, businesses, events or people that once were a part of our lives, or of our parents' and grandparents' lives. Rapid changes during and following World War II affected not only the world but our local culture, leaving familiar landmarks of the '40s, such as neighborhood gas stations and grocery stores, to be repurposed or demolished. An industrial age blossomed and withered during this time span.

We are, once more, grateful to The State Journal-Register for initiating this project to collect images from the Springfield community and to the Sangamon Valley Collection at Lincoln Library for sharing its collection of photographs. This book adds to the treasury of memories documenting the city's development.

Nancy L. Chapin
President
Sangamon County Historical Society

Table of Contents

1940s 7

1950s 53

1960s 115

Business Profiles 158

Index 166

1940s

The nearly 120 photographs in the 1940s chapter of "Springfield Memories Volume II" depict, among many other things, men in uniform preparing to go to war, bowling teams, club activities, people queued up to spend their meat ration coupons or see a free movie, factory assembly lines, and men in uniform returning *from* war.

But perhaps two photos sum up the threat and promise of this schizophrenic decade.

On page 28, 85-year-old Mrs. Mary Watkins of Salisbury holds her "service flag" in 1945. The flag bears 15 blue stars, each denoting one of Watkins' grandchildren or great-grandchildren who had served in World War II. In the middle of the flag is a single gold star — representing Paul Dabney, who was killed in the war.

In the 1940s, central Illinois and the nation had barely climbed out of the Great Depression when the country was immediately plunged into the horror of the world war.

Yet even in the midst of economic and world crises, area residents looked optimistically toward the future, a future embodied in a photo on page 11: five babies, among the winners of a "New Year's Babies" contest, who were born at St. John's Hospital on Jan. 1, 1940.

By the end of the decade, as a beaming majorette confirmed at the 1949 Illinois State Fair, the optimists turned out to be right.

LEFT: National Champ, Rex Mays, in his rally car at the Illinois State Fair, 1947. *Courtesy Jennifer Hendricks*

ABOVE: Springfield Transportation Company employee photo on Easter, March 24, 1940. Charles "Ducky" Barrow is among the employees and was a mechanic. *Courtesy Kent Barrow*

RIGHT: James Johnson and a War Bonds truck that he drove in the early 1940s. *Courtesy Donna Arnold Catlin*

OPPOSITE TOP: The Community Bakery fleet at 1131-35 West Governor Street, circa 1940. *Courtesy Sangamon Valley Collection, Lincoln Library*

OPPOSITE BOTTOM LEFT: The Elks Club building at 509 South Sixth Street in the 1940s. *Courtesy Sangamon Valley Collection, Lincoln Library*

OPPOSITE BOTTOM RIGHT: Central Illinois Light Co. bowling team, circa 1940. First person on left is Herman George Kuntzman. *Courtesy Dorothy Babich*

ABOVE: Citizen Tribune Newspaper carriers, late 1940s. Identified are Dale Hunter, circulation manager; Malcom Adams, editor; and Carl Rudin, general manager. *Courtesy Dale Hunter*

RIGHT: Illinois State Journal building, March 1940. *Courtesy The State-Journal Register*

FAR RIGHT: Bystanders watch as an ambulance arrives at the St. Nicholas Hotel alleyway in the 1940s. *Courtesy Sangamon Valley Collection, Lincoln Library*

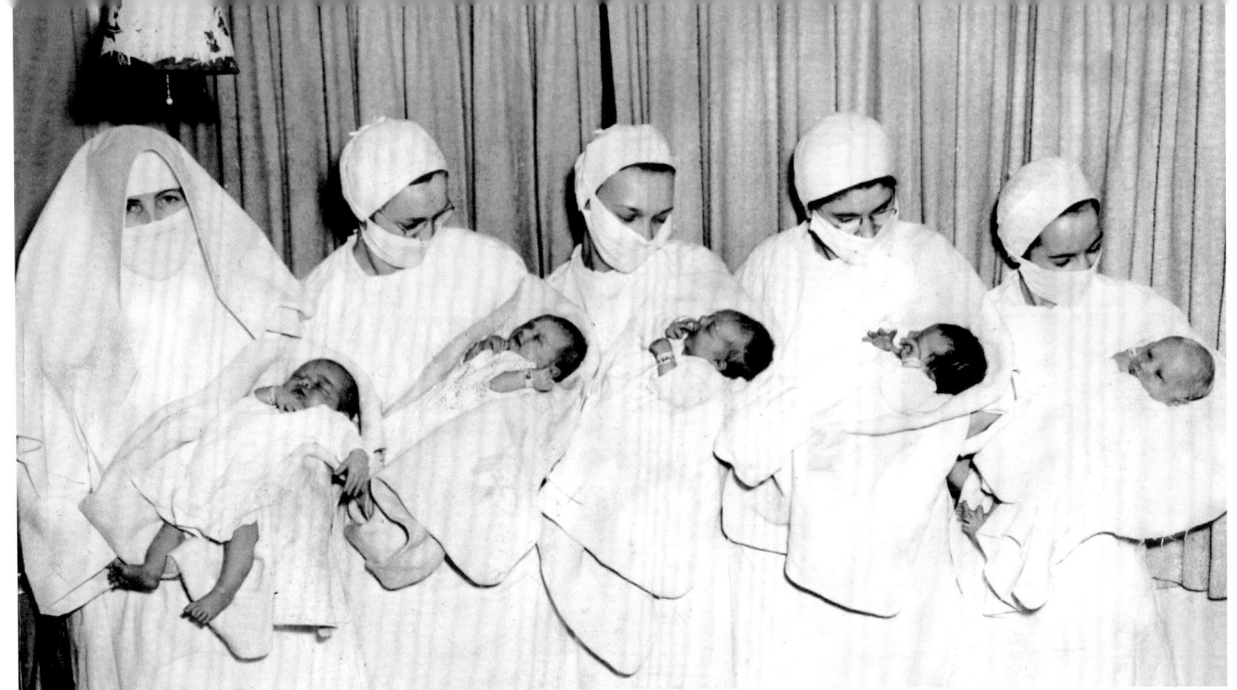

ABOVE: A view of the U.S. Marine Band in the walkway in front of the Sangamon County Courthouse, currently the Old State Capitol, 1940. *Courtesy Nadine Springer*

BELOW: Peter Lou in his World War II uniform, circa 1940. *Courtesy Beverly J. Helm-Renfro*

ABOVE: The "New Year's Babies" born on January 1, 1940 at St. John's Hospital. From the left, the babies pictured were born to the following parents: Mr. and Mrs. Robert Ewald, Mr. and Mrs. Alphonse F. Fleming Jr., Mr. and Mrs. Nicholas Longen, Mr. and Mrs. Edgar Pierce, and Mr. and Mrs. Harold Hollis. The nurses identified holding the babies are Mary Griswold, Betty Peciokas, Rebecca Ford and Rita Zohlen. Prizes were given by the Illinois State Register and 17 Springfield merchants to the first 10 babies born in Springfield in 1940. *Courtesy Dylan Shomidie*

BELOW: Springfield Fire Department Firehouse No. 5, located at 1310 East Adams Street, was the only all-black firehouse in Springfield. *Courtesy Beverly J. Helm-Renfro*

ABOVE: Bulk agent for Cities Service Oil Co., George Wieland, on the left, with another fellow, 11th Street and what is now Stevenson Drive, circa 1940. *Courtesy Donna Wieland Carver*

TOP LEFT: The Canselar family farm on Eighth Street, late 1940s. *Courtesy Beverly J. Helm-Renfro*

LEFT: A group of men fishing off the dam at the Vachel Lindsay Bridge, circa 1940. *Courtesy Alfred G. Dudda and Linda Dudda Dickerson*

OPPOSITE: Poultry judging at the Illinois State Fair in the early 1940s. *Courtesy Sangamon Valley Collection, Lincoln Library*

RIGHT: The interior of May Bordan's Tavern, circa 1940. *Courtesy Betty Bordan*

FAR RIGHT: Eldon and Elizabeth "Betty" Gedney visiting the Beach House at Lake Springfield, May 5, 1940. *Courtesy Kathy Gedney Speder*

BOTTOM RIGHT: Interior view of a Christmas dinner party held in the Abraham Lincoln Hotel in the 1940s. *Courtesy Sangamon Valley Collection, Lincoln Library*

OPPOSITE: Interior view of Graham's Restaurant and Cigar Store during Christmas 1940. *Courtesy Sangamon Valley Collection, Lincoln Library*

BELOW: Waitresses lined up behind the bar at the Palm Room at Eighth and Washington streets, circa 1940. *Courtesy Beverly J. Helm-Renfro*

ABOVE: Bear's Shoe Shop at 18th and Washington streets, circa 1940. *Courtesy Beverly J. Helm-Renfro*

LEFT: Tent City where John Hay Homes were built, circa 1940. *Courtesy Beverly J. Helm-Renfro*

FAR LEFT: Fleck's Airport on Old Rochester Road, circa 1940. George H. Wieland was the distributor for the fuel for the airport. *Courtesy Donna Wieland Carver*

ABOVE: Skating Regulars Club at the Silver Leaf Roller Rink on Washington Street, circa 1940. Identified is Wilma Murray Dudda, who is the sixth in from the right. *Courtesy Wilma Murray Dudda and Linda Dudda Dickerson*

OPPOSITE: A group of girls and two boys all dressed up for dance class, late 1940s. On the top left is Yvonne Hashman. *Courtesy Yvonne Ahrens*

BELOW: Members of the Springfield Urban League, which was located where the Boys & Girls Clubs of Springfield stands today, late 1940s. *Courtesy Beverly J. Helm-Renfro*

ABOVE: Group of women from a local dance group, circa 1940s. Identified is Loretta Shomidie, second from the right. *Courtesy Dylan Shomidie*

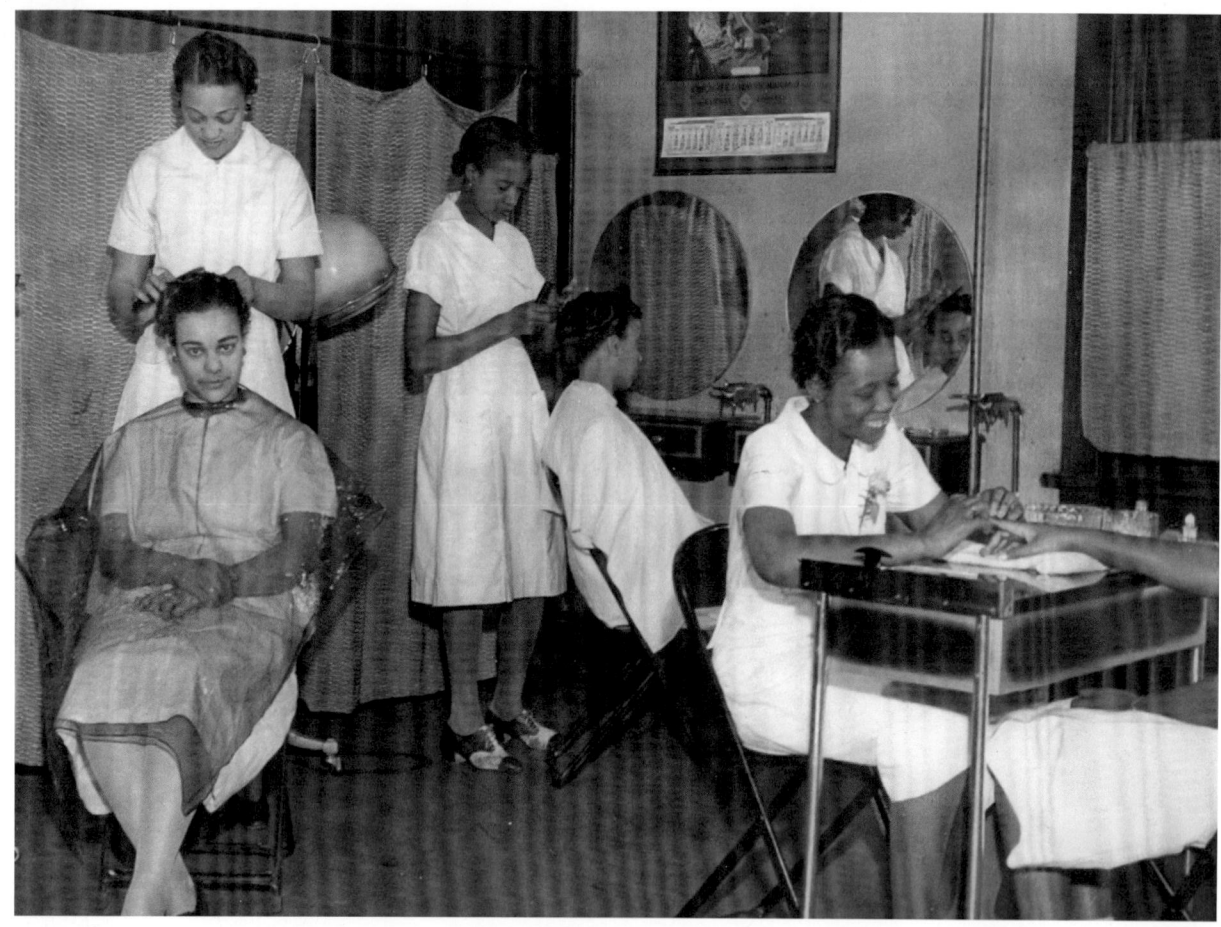

ABOVE: Gorens' School of Beauty Culture student demonstration in 1940. *Courtesy Julia Ann Shultz*

TOP RIGHT: Floyd Thompson and his dog "Snooky" at their home on South Eighth Street, 1941. *Courtesy Kory Koviski*

RIGHT: Gorens' School of Beauty Culture in 1940. *Courtesy Julia Ann Shultz*

OPPOSITE: Students of Harvard Park Elementary School, 2500 Yale Boulevard, 1942. In the photo are Robert Babiak, Walter Babiak, David Beatty, Louise Bell, Frank Bennett, Richard Blalock, Lucille Boggs, Mary Bose, Ina Brawner, Paul Brown, Wayne Brown, Virginia Burns, Scott Clark, James Croft, Robert Davenport, Donald Davis, Dan Edwards, Shirley Ellis, Betty Furrow, William Griffith, Mildred Hanner, Patricia Heger, Donald Hoelzel, Gerry Hubbard, Harold Kane, Mary Lee Kincaid, Alvin Krell Jr., Clifford Langenfeld, John Lauterback, Lum Leach Jr., William Miller, William Moore, Robert Neathery, Betty Peters, Gene Riley, Imogene Riley, Dale Robinson, Shirley Sakris, Donald Smith, Russell Spindel, Norma Sullivan, Georgeene Sweisberger and John Wood. *Courtesy Marjorie and Alvin Krell Jr.*

ABOVE: The Carver family, 1942. From left are, Henry Carver, Mae Carver Fuess, John Carver, Chester Carver, and Etta Carver. *Courtesy Carolyn Morrison*

TOP: Group photo of the Shomidie children, 1942. From left is George, age 13; Barbara, age 12; Loretta, age 14; and Bill, age 15. *Courtesy Dylan Shomidie*

RIGHT: Fire at Liberty Cleaners at 108 North Fifth Street on January 31, 1941. *Courtesy Sangamon Valley Collection, Lincoln Library*

ABOVE: Employees of the Lincoln Ordnance Depot, 1942. Identified is Gene Gilmore, who worked for the fire department. *Courtesy Sherrell Gilmore Petrella*

LEFT: People line up on Monroe Street between Fifth and Sixth streets waiting for Monroe Street Market to open so they could purchase meat with ration coupons in 1943. *Courtesy Sangamon Valley Collection, Lincoln Library*

BELOW: The Russel Dean family portable popcorn stand, 1942. *Courtesy Alice Dean Reynolds*

ABOVE: Capital City Lodge 1160 parade marshal car driven by Jack Gorens 1943. *Courtesy Julia Ann Shultz*

TOP RIGHT: Susan Ostermeier with her grandfather, George Webster, getting ready to show her Guernsey heifer in the 4-H show at the Illinois State Fair in 1943. *Courtesy Susan Ostermeier Tesar*

RIGHT: A view of the flooded street at Fifth and Broad streets, May 18, 1943. The viaduct did not drain quickly enough to keep the street from flooding. *Courtesy Cynthia Olson*

OPPOSITE: Fry cook Paul Burk demonstrates how hot the temperature was on that day by frying an egg on the iron grate outside on the corner of Sixth and Washington streets, 1943. *Courtesy Susan Burk*

ABOVE: Donna Dowson, 14, of Springfield, samples the icing on the decorated birthday cake that helped her win the "Cook of Tomorrow" title at the Illinois State Fair for the second consecutive year in the 1940s. *Courtesy Sangamon Valley Collection, Lincoln Library*

TOP: The Reason Buick Company building at 310 South Second Street, circa 1945 *Courtesy Sangamon Valley Collection, Lincoln Library*

RIGHT: C. Duane Lambert out on his newspaper route with his dog, "Skipper," on 507 South Walnut Street, 1944. The dog even had his own small wooden seat on the front of the bike. *Courtesy Rose Marie Lambert*

ABOVE: James Hyatt in his uniform, after coming home from Africa during World Ward II, 1944. *Courtesy Sharon McMullen*

LEFT: Portrait of Donald Blake in his U.S. Army uniform, 1944. *Courtesy Joyce Stroble Stuper*

FAR LEFT: Donald Towsley, left, and Chick Capin, "Hangar Flying" during their Civil Air Patrol training at the Springfield Southwest Airport, 1944. The aircraft was a Stinson Reliant. *Courtesy Martin Towsley*

ABOVE: Springfield residents crowd the streets to celebrate the end of World War II in August 1945. View of Fifth and Monroe streets looking southwest. *Courtesy Sangamon Valley Collection, Lincoln Library*

TOP LEFT: Marilyn Zanders Stalets and her father Joseph Zanders in front of the family home at 839 North Eighth Street, 1945. *Courtesy Marilyn Zanders Stalets*

FAR TOP LEFT: Jim Dalbey and his son, David Dalbey, 4, May 1945. *Courtesy David Dalbey*

BOTTOM LEFT: Troops returning from Europe in 1945. *Courtesy Julia Ann Shultz*

OPPOSITE: Mary Watkins of Salisbury, 85, displays her service flag with 15 blue stars and one gold star, circa 1945. This represented the 11 grandchildren and 4 great-grandchildren in the service. The gold star represented Paul B. Dabney, who was killed in action in Italy. *Courtesy Karla Krueger*

ABOVE: A group of singers gathers around the piano for a singing competition at the Illinois State Fair in the 1940s. *Courtesy Sangamon Valley Collection, Lincoln Library*

TOP RIGHT: Junior department girls receive their ribbons for dressmaking at the Illinois State Fair in the 1940s. *Courtesy Sangamon Valley Collection, Lincoln Library*

MIDDLE RIGHT: A few of the Reynolds children — Frank, age 10; Shirley, age 8; Beverly, age 6; David, age 3; and Velma, age 2 — pose together on a Packard car, Spaulding Road, 1946. This was only five of the 13 Reynolds children. *Courtesy Virginia Patton*

RIGHT: Bystanders gather outside the YWCA at Fifth and Jackson streets as firefighters rush to put out a fire, circa 1945. *Courtesy Sangamon Valley Collection, Lincoln Library*

ABOVE: State commanders of various war veterans groups gather at the Executive Mansion with Gov. Adlai E. Stevenson prior to opening Veterans Day festivities at the Illinois State Fair, late '40s. From left: are Warren Neureither, commander of the Spanish American War Veterans; Merle E. Schaad, department commander of the American Legion; James R. Schmitz, commander of the state Veterans of Foreign Wars; Gov. Stevenson; Charles E. Cessna Jr., department commander of the Disabled American Veterans; Walter T. Popjoy, commandant of the Illinois Squadron of Navy Clubs; and Ray Byers, superintendent of Veterans Day. The last man is unidentified. *Courtesy Sangamon Valley Collection, Lincoln Library*

TOP LEFT: The Illinois State Fair management entertained 35 students of the St. James Trade School in the 1940s. Among the group are William C. Henry; Brother Serapicon, an instructor at the school; and Brother Nicetius. *Courtesy Sangamon Valley Collection, Lincoln Library*

LEFT: A.R. Kays, administrator of the Illinois Veterans Commission, explains the commission's exhibit to Gov. Adlai E. Stevenson at the "Your Illinois" tented display at the Illinois State Fair, late '40s.
Courtesy Sangamon Valley Collection, Lincoln Library

ABOVE: Executive Board and Labor Relations Committee, Flour Mill Workers Union Local 21101, August 1945. *Courtesy Joyce Stroble Stuper*

TOP LEFT: Mayor Harry Eielson gathers with a group of women to honor Abraham Lincoln in the 1940s. *Courtesy Sangamon Valley Collection, Lincoln Library*

BOTTOM LEFT: Signing of the Airport Authorities Act that established Capital Airport, April 4, 1945. Present at the signing were A.L. Sargent, executive director; Louis Rodier, labor official; Henry M. Lutz, chairman; George C. Roberts, secretary of Illinois Aeronautics Commission; Hugh J. Dobbs, attorney; Hugh W. Cross, lieutenant governor; J. David Jones, Junior Chamber of Commerce; Sen. Charles F. Carpentier of Rock Island County (later Illinois State Secretary of State); Robert R. Edwards, member of the Aviation Committee; Sen. John W. Fribley; Sen. D. Logan Giffen; Sen. Everett R. Peters; Sen. Martin B. Lohman; Carl Swienfurth, president of the Illinois State Chamber of Commerce; Clarence B. Chiles, Illinois Aeronautics Commission; John E. Sankey Sr., Springfield Chamber of Commerce; John W. Kapp Jr., mayor of Springfield; and Gov. Dwight H. Green. *Courtesy Jim Lutz*

OPPOSITE: Interior view of the production line inside Allis-Chalmers warehouse in 1945. *Courtesy Sangamon Valley Collection, Lincoln Library*

33

ABOVE: The Satchel Paige baseball team is visited by their namesake, baseball great Satchel Paige, at Lanphier Park, 1946. From left to right, first row: Satchel Paige, Charles Isom (wearing white cap, partially hidden behind Paige), Raymond Henry, Kenneth Brown, Joe Hughes, Monroe Banks, Leonard Hubbard, Enos Brents (only top portion of his face is visible), and Mr. Coleman. Second row: Jimmie Watson, Bobby Gorens, Rudy Boswell, Frank Robinson, Cedell Chaney. Third row: Clarence Senor, Ozzie Banks, William Gilbert, Paul Hammons, and Dick Tate, manager. The young boy in front is unidentified. *Courtesy Clarence Senor*

BELOW: Race car driver Jack Horn, accepting the trophy for national champion of the 100-mile auto race, Illinois State Fair, 1946. The man identified to his right is John Hobbs. *Courtesy Jennifer Hendricks*

ABOVE: The first Salvation Army Girls Softball Team, 1945. Identified are, first row: Dorothy Paoni, Toni Galassi, Trillie Galassi Huffman, and Dorothy Gentry. Second row: Liz Gillock and Louise "Beja" Caprinica. Third row: coach Fred Paoni, Helen Quinnigan Duffy and Kathleen "Babe" Paoni Evans. *Courtesy Kathleen "Babe" Paoni Evans*

BELOW: First Communion class at St. Aloysius Church, July 1945. *Courtesy Joyce Stroble Stuper*

ABOVE: The Ostermeier family reunion at Washington Park in 1946. *Courtesy Susan Ostermeier Tesar*

LEFT: View of traffic on the east side of Sixth Street between Adams and Monroe streets, circa 1947. *Courtesy Sangamon Valley Collection, Lincoln Library*

BELOW: Springfieldians and other Illinois residents gather at a beer tent at the Illinois State Fair in 1947. The beer tents were banned under the William G. Stratton administration between 1953 and 1961. Prior to the Stratton administration, beer was sold at the fair. Under the administrations that followed, beer tents were not permitted at the fair, but fair-goers were known to bring their own amber-colored beverages for refreshment. *Courtesy Sangamon Valley Collection, Lincoln Library*

ABOVE: The first Christmas meeting for the Unique Matronettes Club in 1947. Among those known are Emma Moore, Gloria Jackson, Cecelia White and Virginia Scott. *Courtesy Sangamon Valley Collection, Lincoln Library*

BELOW: View of customers in line for a free Saturday morning show at the Lincoln Theater in 1947.
Courtesy Sangamon Valley Collection, Lincoln Library

ABOVE: Meadow Gold ice cream delivery trucks lined up in front of the Illinois Dairy in 1947. *Courtesy Sangamon Valley Collection, Lincoln Library*

OPPOSITE: The Springfield Sepian Club, circa 1947. *Courtesy Sangamon Valley Collection, Lincoln Library*

BELOW: View of Seventh and Monroe streets in 1947. In the foreground is the city hall and immediately behind is Firehouse No. 1. The post office lawn is to the right. *Courtesy Sangamon Valley Collection, Lincoln Library*

37

ABOVE: Pillsbury Mills in September of 1947. *Courtesy Sangamon Valley Collection, Lincoln Library*

RIGHT: Stacks of canned goods and spices in the Kelly Brothers Grocery Store, 1947. *Courtesy Gail Kelly*

ABOVE: The Champion Service Station at 1101 West Jefferson Street, circa 1947. The station was owned by Jesse Warner and leased by George Rees. At the time of the photo a railroad station was located behind the station where Madison Avenue runs through today. *Courtesy Tyre Rees*

BELOW: Display of the meat counter in the Kelly Brothers Grocery Store, 1947. Jay Kelly is in the apron behind the counter. *Courtesy Gail Kelly*

ABOVE: Wedding photo of Boyce W. Pickett to Patricia Cook, September 28, 1947. From left are Carol Kemp, Tom Kemp, Boyce W. Pickett, Patricia (Cook) Pickett, Helen Stroble, Eleanor DeYoung, and Marjorie Cook. *Courtesy Marjorie and Alvin Krell Jr.*

LEFT: Interior of the St. Francis of Assisi Church at the Motherhouse of the Hospital Sisters of St. Francis. The church was designed by Helmle and Helmle. *Courtesy Brian Blasio*

BELOW: First communion for the children of Sacred Heart School on May 11, 1947. *Courtesy Dylan Shomidie*

ABOVE: Pleasant Hill School fourth-grade class photo, 1948. Identified in front, from left: Joe Tomlin, Jim (last name unknown), Jack Barlow, unidentified and Jim Holtzworth. Second row: Mary Rose Barlow, Mary Jane Woods, Joann Sargeant Blake, unidentified, Joann Croll, Verna Harlan, Marilyn Lou Lane, Nancy Peontel, Susanne Foster and Patsy Krska. Third row: Ronald Barrow, Vincent Cousin, Larry Collins, David Greenfield, Raymond Giao, Harvey Blake, David Burris, Joe Tomlin, David Medley, Bruce Barrow, and Jim Watkins. Back row: Mrs. Kinney, David (last name unknown), John O'Dell, unidentified, Frank Fishburn, Carolyn Hunter, Evelyn Beard, Joann Coe, Joyce Petschauer, Joann Jarvis, Carolyn Barrow, Mary Myers, Ellen Woods, and Mr. Mennis. *Courtesy Marilyn Lane*

40

ABOVE: Exterior of Paris Cleaners at Eleventh and Ash streets, circa 1948. *Courtesy Sangamon Valley Collection, Lincoln Library*

LEFT: Gov. Dwight Green, seen leaning against the counter, stands amidst the women of the Dairy Building at the Illinois State Fair, circa 1948. *Courtesy Sangamon Valley Collection, Lincoln Library*

BOTTOM LEFT: Cold participants gather near the Abraham Lincoln Friendship Train for a ceremony, February 1948. *Courtesy Sangamon Valley Collection, Lincoln Library*

BELOW: An Abraham Lincoln impersonator stands at the back of the Abraham Lincoln Friendship Train, February 1948. *Courtesy Sangamon Valley Collection, Lincoln Library*

ABOVE: Roseburg Brothers Sinclair Station at 900 North Grand Avenue East, circa 1948. *Courtesy Sangamon Valley Collection, Lincoln Library*

TOP: The United States Marine Corps band pays a visit to the Illinois Capitol in 1948. *Courtesy Sangamon Valley Collection, Lincoln Library*

TOP RIGHT: Mayor Buddy Kapp, striped suit, at the C & A Station, early 1940s. *Courtesy Sangamon Valley Collection, Lincoln Library*

RIGHT: Customers line up around the block for the grand opening of the new Spiegel Store on the north side of East Washington Street between Fourth and Fifth streets in 1948. *Courtesy Sangamon Valley Collection, Lincoln Library*

OPPOSITE: Lake Springfield Christian Assembly High School Week, June 1948. *Courtesy Sangamon Valley Collection, Lincoln Library*

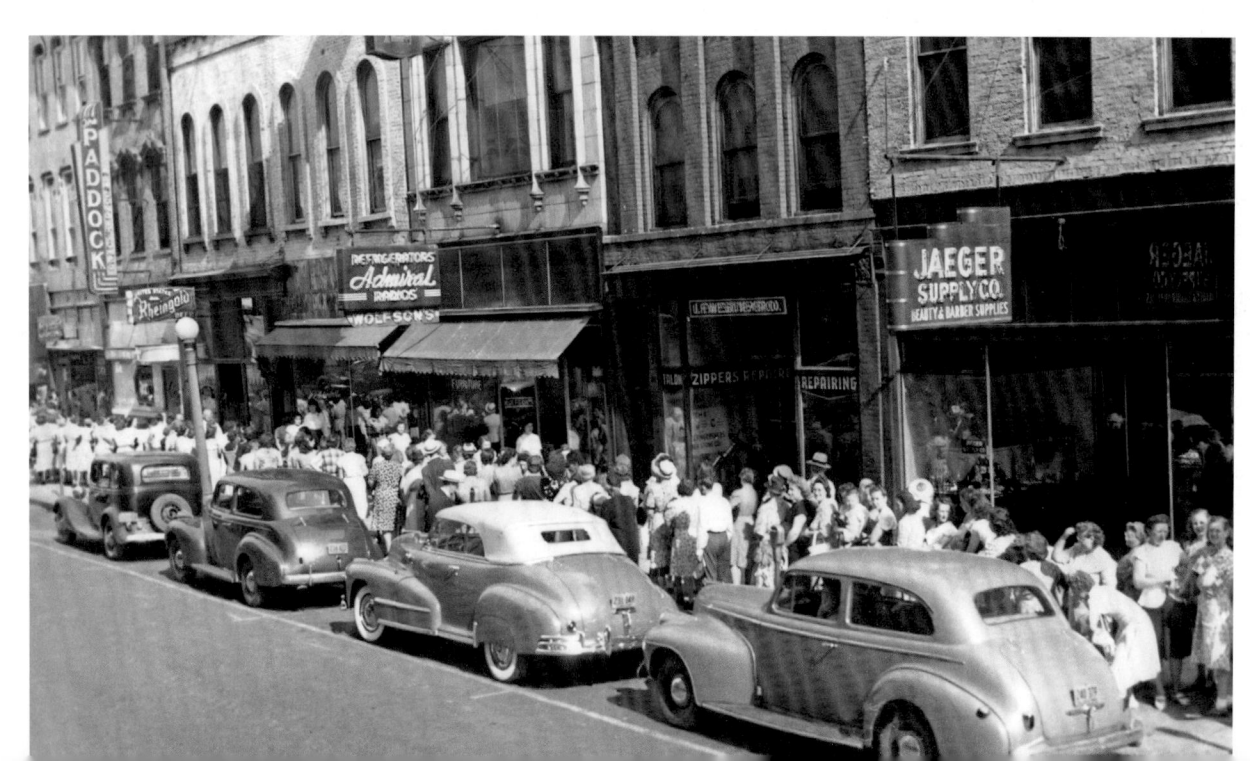

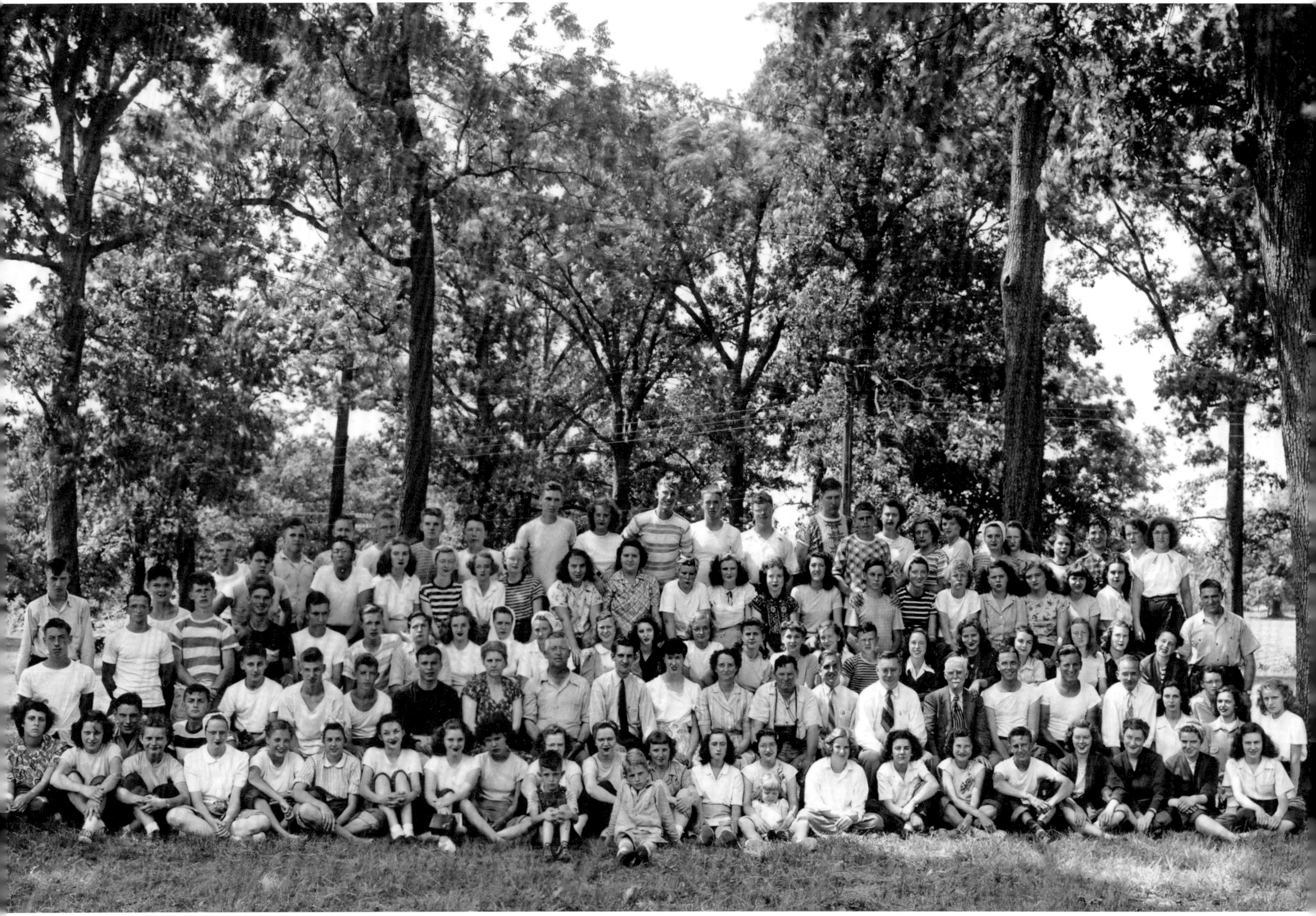

ABOVE: Floral Hall building at the Illinois State Fair, 1948. *Courtesy Sangamon Valley Collection, Lincoln Library*

TOP RIGHT: The Fulgenzi family outside their residence at 2112 North Sixth Street, circa 1948. From left is Ferdy Fulgenzi, Donna Fulgenzi, Darlene Fulgenzi, Adolfo Fulgenzi, Margaret Fulgenzi and Jimmy Fulgenzi. *Courtesy Margaret Sauer and Karen Brooks*

BOTTOM RIGHT: View of St. Nicholas Hotel, circa 1948. *Courtesy Sangamon Valley Collection, Lincoln Library*

BELOW: The Women's Association of Officers and Circle Leaders at Westminster Presbyterian Church, 1948. *Courtesy Westminster Presbyterian Church*

ABOVE: John H. Wilson Jr. in front of a Tucker car that was used in a Springfield parade, 1948. *Courtesy Shirley Wilson*

BELOW: Illinois State Fair parking lot, next to the home of Charles and Sofie Meiron, circa 1948. Seated in chairs from left are, Helen Meiron, Sofie Meiron and Betty Meiron Ritter. *Courtesy Margaret Hohimer*

ABOVE: John Stuper during an Illinois State Police search maneuvers session at Lake Springfield, August 1949. *Courtesy Lisa Agusti*

BELOW: Building on the southwest corner of Sixth and Adams streets, May 30, 1949. The building was erected by Seth Tinsley and housed the law offices of Lincoln and Herndon. *Courtesy Judith Barringer*

ABOVE: View looking south on Fifth Street from Jefferson Street, circa 1948. *Courtesy Sangamon Valley Collection, Lincoln Library*

TOP RIGHT: Aftermath of a collapsed wall at 417 East Monroe Street on January 26, 1949. *Courtesy Sangamon Valley Collection, Lincoln Library*

RIGHT: The visit of President Harry Truman in 1948. From left are State Rep. Paul Powell, President Harry Truman, U.S. Sen. Scott Lucas and Secretary of State Edward Barrett. *Courtesy Sangamon Valley Collection, Lincoln Library*

OPPOSITE: View of Second Street, October 1949. Buildings seen from left are the Capital Way Inn, a service station and Penewitt Buick. *Courtesy Sangamon Valley Collection, Lincoln Library*

47

ABOVE: Gov. Adlai E. Stevenson gathers with a group of women at the Illinois State Fair for a photo, circa 1949. *Courtesy Sangamon Valley Collection, Lincoln Library*

TOP RIGHT: Mary Ann Meyer, a 17-year-old majorette from Golf, Ill., is presented with the Governor's Trophy after she won first place in the 1949 Illinois State Fair twirling contest. Presenting the trophy is G.W. Patrick of Springfield, superintendent of the contest. *Courtesy Sangamon Valley Collection, Lincoln Library*

RIGHT: Mark Hewitt, student at Roosevelt High School in Chicago, demonstrates carving plastics in the Chicago Public School Industrial Arts exhibit at the Illinois State Fair, circa 1949. Looking over his shoulder is his father, Coleman Hewitt, instructor at Chicago Teachers College, who was in charge of the exhibit. A.B. McCall, with cap, of Springfield, was the supervisor of the school exhibits at the time. *Courtesy Sangamon Valley Collection, Lincoln Library*

ABOVE: Turning in the fastest qualifying mile in the AMA motorcycle racing program at the Illinois State Fair in 1949 is Paul Albrecht. He toured the mile oval in 44:13 seconds. *Courtesy Sangamon Valley Collection, Lincoln Library*

TOP LEFT: Gov. Adlai E. Stevenson opens Veterans Day at the Illinois State Fair in 1949.
Courtesy Sangamon Valley Collection, Lincoln Library

LEFT: Gov. Adlai E. Stevenson turns over the keys to the new family car to Harold Calkins, an Ottawa farmer, whose family was judged the Illinois Typical Farm Family of 1949 at the Illinois State Fair in 1949. Standing before the shiny new Ford, which was the grand prize in the state contest, are 15-year-old Mary Lou, left, Mrs. Calkins, and, to the far right, 19-year-old Charles. The Calkins family was the victor over 11 families entered in the contest by newspapers throughout the state. *Courtesy Sangamon Valley Collection, Lincoln Library*

RIGHT: The Sacred Heart Grade School basketball team, 1949, had a successful season with 18 consecutive games won. Top row, from left, are Joe Lepper, Richard Fix, Jim Vose, Bill Adelman and Bill Garecht. In the second row are the Rev. Luke Kelly, Bernie Lindsay, David Teer, Mike Aiello, Bob Martin, Don Hays, George Ramelow, coach Leo McGrath and the Rev. John Brockmeier. In the front row are Margaret Gramlich, Theresa Rock, Maryann DeBeaulieu, Carol McNally, Sara Bristow, Pat Daley and Niece Power, mascot. *Courtesy Sangamon Valley Collection, Lincoln Library*

BOTTOM RIGHT: The Leland Hotel, circa 1949. *Courtesy Sangamon Valley Collection, Lincoln Library*

BELOW: View of Jefferson Street looking east from Fourth Street in 1949. Seen here are the Hotel Empire, International Business Machines, The Revel, Red Top Cabs and the St. Nicholas Hotel. *Courtesy Sangamon Valley Collection, Lincoln Library*

ABOVE: Sixteen local dancers of the Sansone Studio at the Orpheum Theater, 1949. Identified are S. Reagan, M.J. Johnson, S. Ray, B. Monohan, U.R. Hutton, N. Bartlett, D. Winstead, N. Winstead, P. Brancato, P. Delaney, S. Wilson, and V. Jackson. The dancers were doing a line dance to "I'm Looking Over a Four Leaf Clover." *Courtesy Patricia J. Delaney Murawski*

LEFT: May Bordan leaning on her car outside of May Bordan's Tavern on the west side of Old Route 66 near what is Riverside Park, 1949. *Courtesy Betty Bordan*

FAR LEFT: The South Town Theatre featuring two shows: "How Green Was My Valley" and "Let's Live Again," July 1949. *Courtesy Sangamon Valley Collection, Lincoln Library*

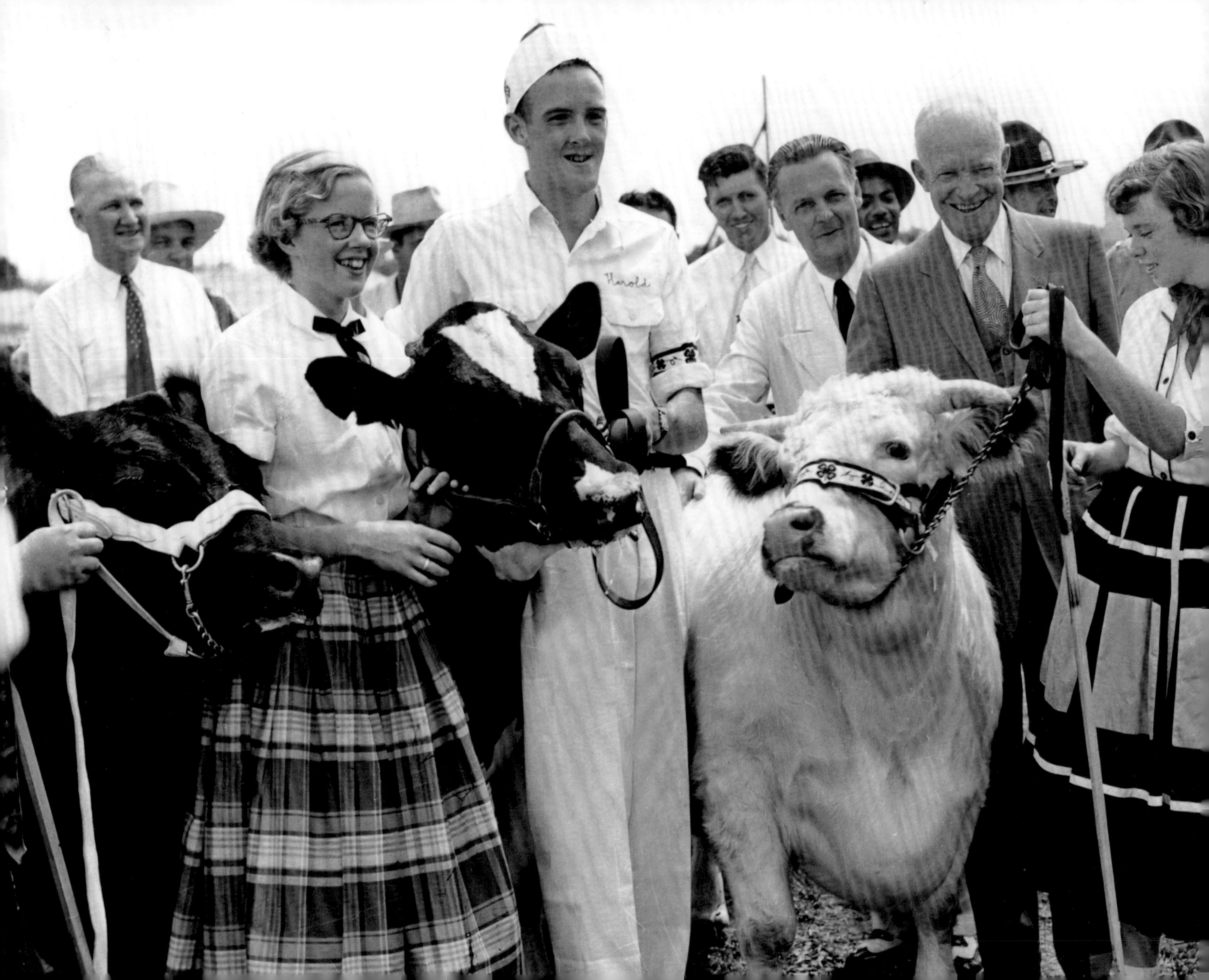
Harold

1950s

The 1950s were a period of innovation in Springfield. WICS-Channel 20 went on the air, Illinois Bell branched out into color telephones, home freezers were "the key to finer living," air conditioning was installed in local office buildings, and Scotchwash laundromats boasted tartan carpeting.

Central Illinois also was developing around Springfield. New subdivisions sprung up. The Inn of the Lampliter got a modest start on the city's south edge. And even farther out, residents of a tiny, rural suburb saw a need for a new high school — Chatham Glenwood, which today is one of the largest schools in Sangamon County.

As always, though, politics was one of Springfield's most prominent industries. Early in the decade, Adlai Stevenson, governor from 1949 to 1953, twice challenged Dwight Eisenhower for the presidency, and both men became familiar figures to central Illinois residents.

One place where you could count on meeting politicians of all stripes was the Illinois State Fair. The 1954 fair was a banner political year — not only was Ike introduced to the Jepson family's steers (left), but U.S. Sen. Paul Douglas (page 82) drew a crowd that same year by demonstrating a surprisingly adept square dance twirl.

LEFT: President Dwight Eisenhower pays a visit to Springfield during the Illinois State Fair in 1954. From left are Margaret Jepson, Harold Jepson, Gov. William G. Stratton, President Eisenhower, Bonigail Bivin and Gov. George H. Craig of Indiana. *Courtesy Sangamon Valley Collection, Lincoln Library*

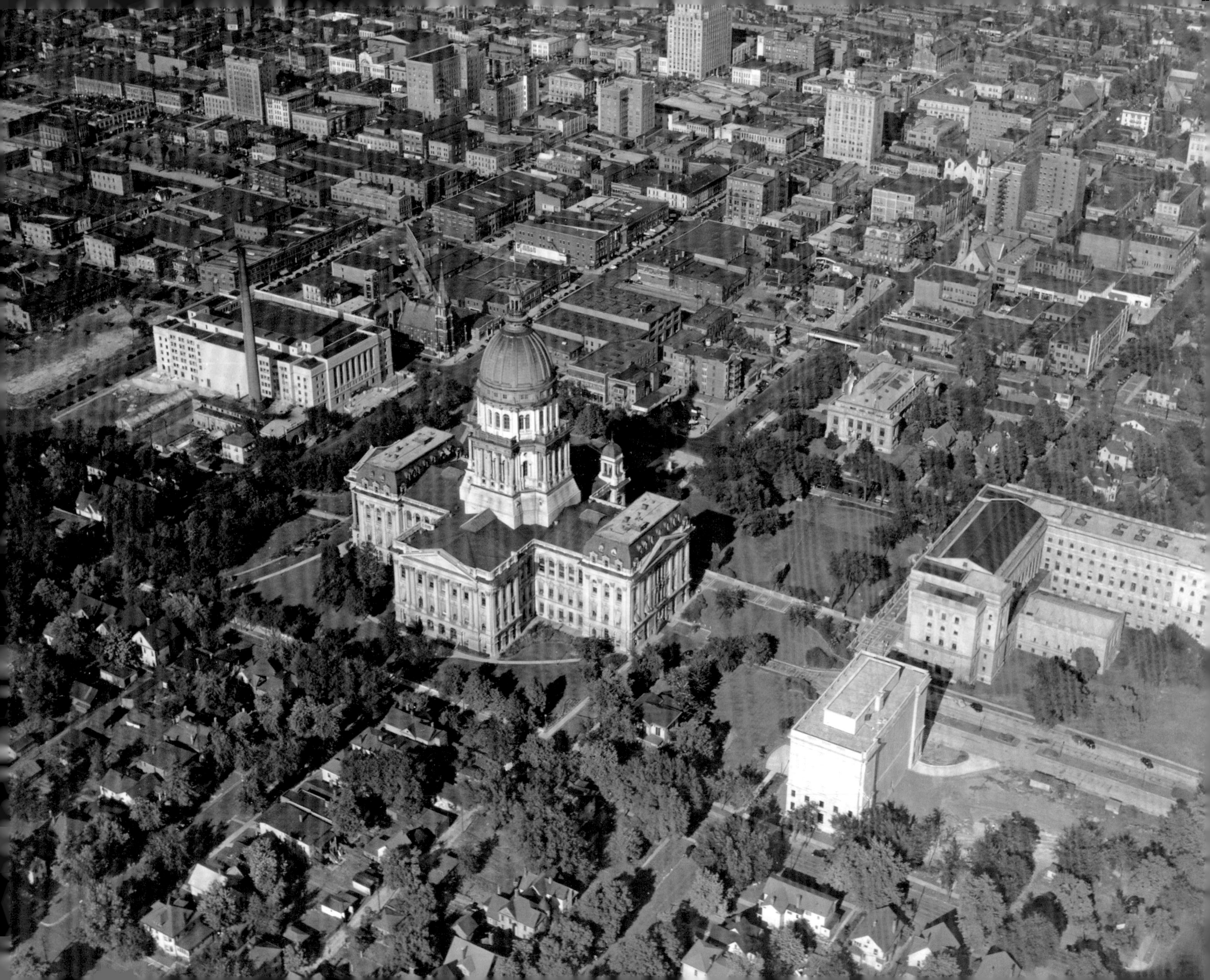

ABOVE: A view from Capitol Avenue looking at the Second Street face of the Capitol. *Courtesy Bill Broderick*

TOP LEFT: The Navy Club at Lake Springfield, circa 1950s. *Courtesy Sangamon Valley Collection, Lincoln Library*

LEFT: The Springfield Municipal Band gathers for a group shot in the Rose Room at St. Nicholas Hotel, May 1950. *Courtesy Sangamon Valley Collection, Lincoln Library*

OPPOSITE: Aerial view of Springfield, circa 1950. *Courtesy Sangamon Valley Collection, Lincoln Library*

ABOVE: Glen and Mabel Miller with their caged layers at the Red and White Farm west of Springfield on Lincoln Trail in the 1950s. *Courtesy Ginger Doyle*

OPPOSITE: Part of the East Moline delegation of Rolle Bolle enthusiasts at the Illinois State Fair are shown determining the results of the roll, circa 1950. Kneeling, from left are Rene Kerschieter, Gerald De Jaegher and William Van De Wiele. Standing from left are August De Keere, Rene Covents, Harry Fontegne, Paul Van Hauwaert and Charles Merci. *Courtesy Sangamon Valley Collection, Lincoln Library*

BELOW: Harness race at the Illinois State Fair, circa 1950. *Courtesy Sangamon Valley Collection, Lincoln Library*

ABOVE: View of Pierce Oil Company at 105 North Second Street in 1950. *Courtesy Sangamon Valley Collection, Lincoln Library*

BELOW: WICS-TV crew filming a demonstration of making cakes, presented by B & Z Bakery, at the Illinois State Fair, circa 1950. *Courtesy Sangamon Valley Collection, Lincoln Library*

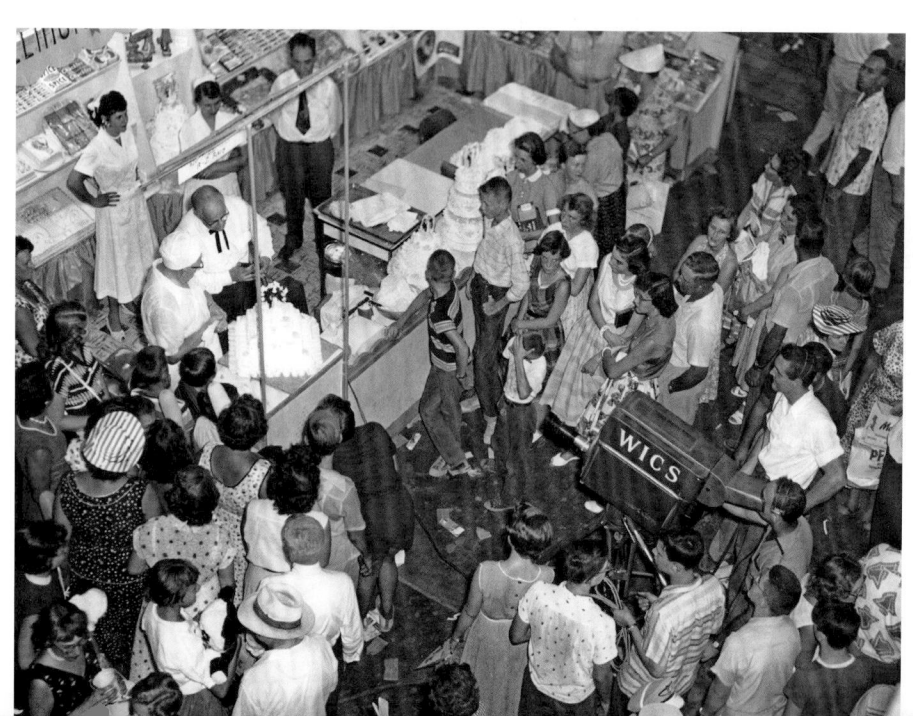

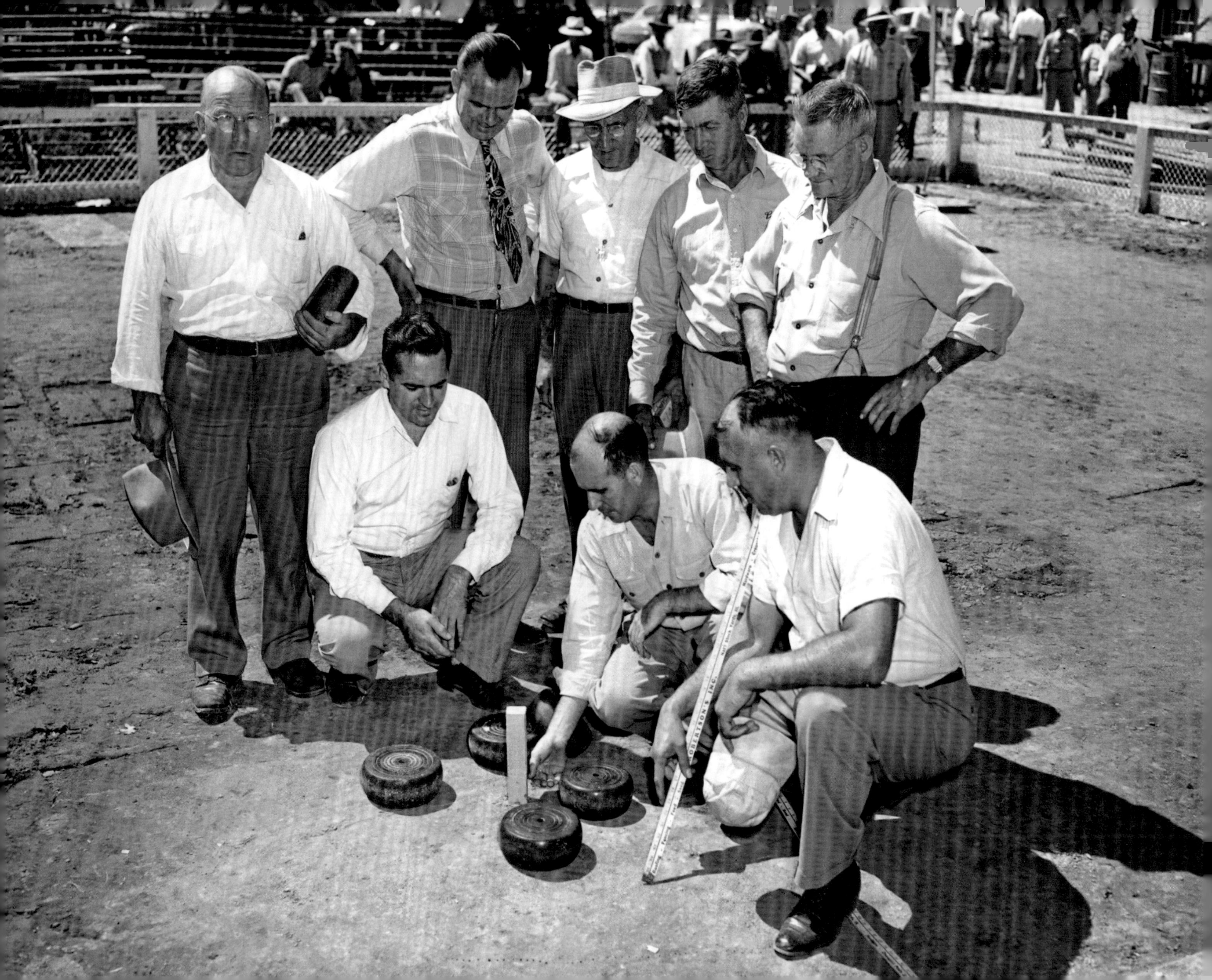
ROBERTSON'S INC.

ABOVE: Chief of detectives James R. McIntyre Sr., third from left, with fellow detectives in front of the Springfield Police Department at 617 East Jefferson Street, 1950. *Courtesy James R. McIntyre Jr.*

BELOW: Members of the Springfield Ceramics and Crafts Club display their projects that were completed in classes throughout the year, circa 1950. From left is Mrs. Fred Luers, Mrs. Geo Cullen, Mrs. Don Lasey, Mrs. J.T. Gourley, and Mrs. A.D. Campbell. *Courtesy Susanne Wall*

ABOVE: Interior view of Connor's, August 1950. *Courtesy Sangamon Valley Collection, Lincoln Library*

BELOW: A dressmaker in her shop, looking over a purchase order, circa 1950. *Courtesy Beverly J. Helm-Renfro*

ABOVE: Dr. Webster, circa 1950. *Courtesy Beverly J. Helm-Renfro*

LEFT: The Grandview Club Reunion, September 1950.
Courtesy Sangamon Valley Collection, Lincoln Library

BELOW: Lampliter Tourist Lodge, August, 4, 1950.
Courtesy Sangamon Valley Collection, Lincoln Library

1 2 3 4 5
6 7 8 9 10 11 12
13 14 15 16 17 18 19
20 21 22 23 24 25 26
27 28 29 30
ALLIS-CHALMERS

ABOVE: Interior of Springfield Brewery, circa 1950. *Courtesy Sangamon Valley Collection, Lincoln Library*

OPPOSITE: Employees at the International Shoe Company, circa 1950. *Courtesy Sangamon Valley Collection, Lincoln Library*

BELOW: Group of sales drivers for Anheuser-Busch company, 1950. *Courtesy Karla Krueger*

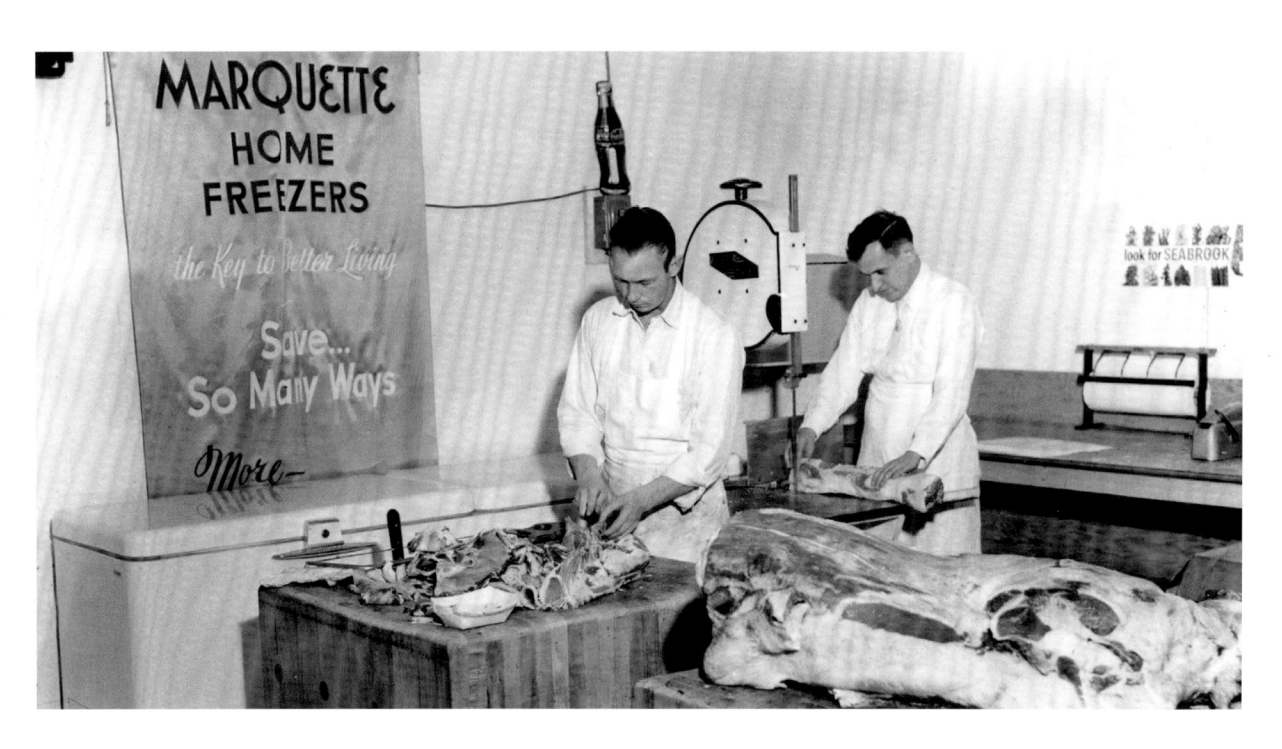

ABOVE: Interior view of La Roi Frozen Foods Company with butchers at work to present the "key to finer living" by freezing food using the Marquette home freezer, circa 1950. *Courtesy Sangamon Valley Collection, Lincoln Library*

BELOW: Exterior of La Roi Frozen Foods Company at 1021 Wabash Avenue, circa 1950. *Courtesy Sangamon Valley Collection, Lincoln Library*

ABOVE: Adjusters Association of Central Illinois fourth annual outing at the Oakcrest Country Club in 1950. *Courtesy Sangamon Valley Collection, Lincoln Library*

BELOW: Firefighters put out the last of the flames at Webb's Corner Tavern at 1418 East Cook Street, circa 1950. *Courtesy Sangamon Valley Collection, Lincoln Library*

ABOVE: Exterior view of Springfield Fire Department Engine House No. 1 at 718-720 East Monroe Street, circa 1950. *Courtesy Sangamon Valley Collection, Lincoln Library*

BELOW: Off-duty firefighters solicited funds for the March of Dimes drive by manning the street corners in the business district in the '40s and '50s. To help publicize the solicitation, firefighters displayed an 1887 steamer and the department's new rig and aerial ladder. *Courtesy Sangamon Valley Collection, Lincoln Library*

ABOVE: Memorial Hospital, circa 1950. *Courtesy Sangamon Valley Collection, Lincoln Library*

BELOW: The east side of the public square with the Sangamon County Courthouse, now the Old State Capitol, on the left, circa 1950. *Courtesy Carolyn Quinlan*

ABOVE: American Ambulance fleet at 1316 South 15th Street in the 1950s. *Courtesy Sangamon Valley Collection, Lincoln Library*

BELOW: Hard at work in the Civil Defense Communications Center in the 1950s. *Courtesy Sangamon Valley Collection, Lincoln Library*

ABOVE: Softball team sponsored by Johnny and Vi's tavern, 1950. Front row, from left: John DeRosa, Bob Frantz, Bill DeRosa, Paul Blush, Raleigh Hinsey, and unknown. In back row, from left: Bob Brust, Bob Flaretty, John Dietel, Mike DeRosa, Joe Krouse, and John Riba, who was the sponsor. *Courtesy Veronica DeRosa*

LEFT: The downtown location of the YMCA on Seventh Street and Capitol Avenue, circa 1950. The building was located across from the Lincoln Library and next to the church Abraham Lincoln attended. *Courtesy Joseph Alan Linder*

BOTTOM LEFT: Janet Cobb, age 4, on a pony in her front yard at 1121 North Franklin Street, 1950. A man with a pony and various outfits made his living going door to door, photographing people on a pony in their front yards. *Courtesy Janet Lea Cobb*

BELOW: Girl Scout Camp Widjiwagan in 1950. Carolyn Quinlan is second from the left, in the back row. *Courtesy Carolyn Quinlan*

ABOVE: Cottage Hill School eighth-grade class graduation photo, circa 1950. Identified in the photo are Kenneth Babich and Jim Gloss, first and second in the back row, on the right and Mike Jones, first on the right in the second row. *Courtesy Dorothy Babich*

ABOVE: The 15th Street Social Club at American Legion Post No. 809 at 12th and Monroe Streets, circa 1950. From left are Mr. and Mrs. Joe Thortons, Mr. and Mrs. Jenkins, Mr. and Mrs. Earl Senor, Mr. and Mrs. Walter Senor, Mr. and Mrs. Chester Dixon, and Mr. and Mrs. Herman Turner. *Courtesy Peggie D. Senor*

TOP RIGHT: Employees of the Pillsbury Co., circa 1950. Identified is Virginia Davis, in the first row on the left side. *Courtesy Dorothy Babich*

RIGHT: The Hummer Manufacturing office on the southeast corner of Ninth Street and South Grand Avenue, circa 1950. Dave Cook is seated at the desk. *Courtesy Marjorie and Alvin Krell, Jr.*

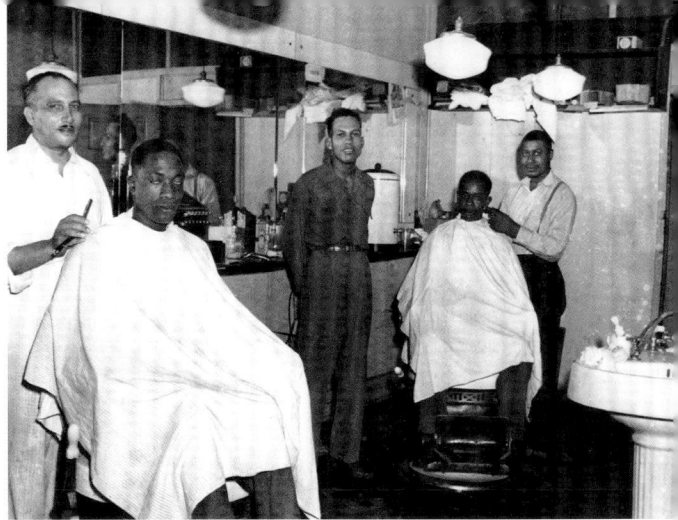

ABOVE: A Girl Scout group at Camp Widjiwagan at Lake Springfield in 1950. The unit leaders were Helen Sellers and Rosabel Rasmussen. *Courtesy Helen Brooks*

TOP: A group of gentlemen getting their hair done at the George Sykes Barber Shop, circa 1950. George Sykes can be seen on the far right. *Courtesy Beverly J. Helm-Renfro*

TOP LEFT: A Union Station cab driver waiting for passengers, early 1950s. *Courtesy Shirley Wilson*

LEFT: Miss Southlawn Shirley (Snodgrass) Sims, left, and Miss Springfield Katie Knox standing in front of the site of the Southlawn subdivision off Stevenson Drive, 1950. Paul Snodgrass, Shirley's father, built the first home in the Southlawn subdivision in 1940. *Courtesy Barabara R. Piiparinen*

67

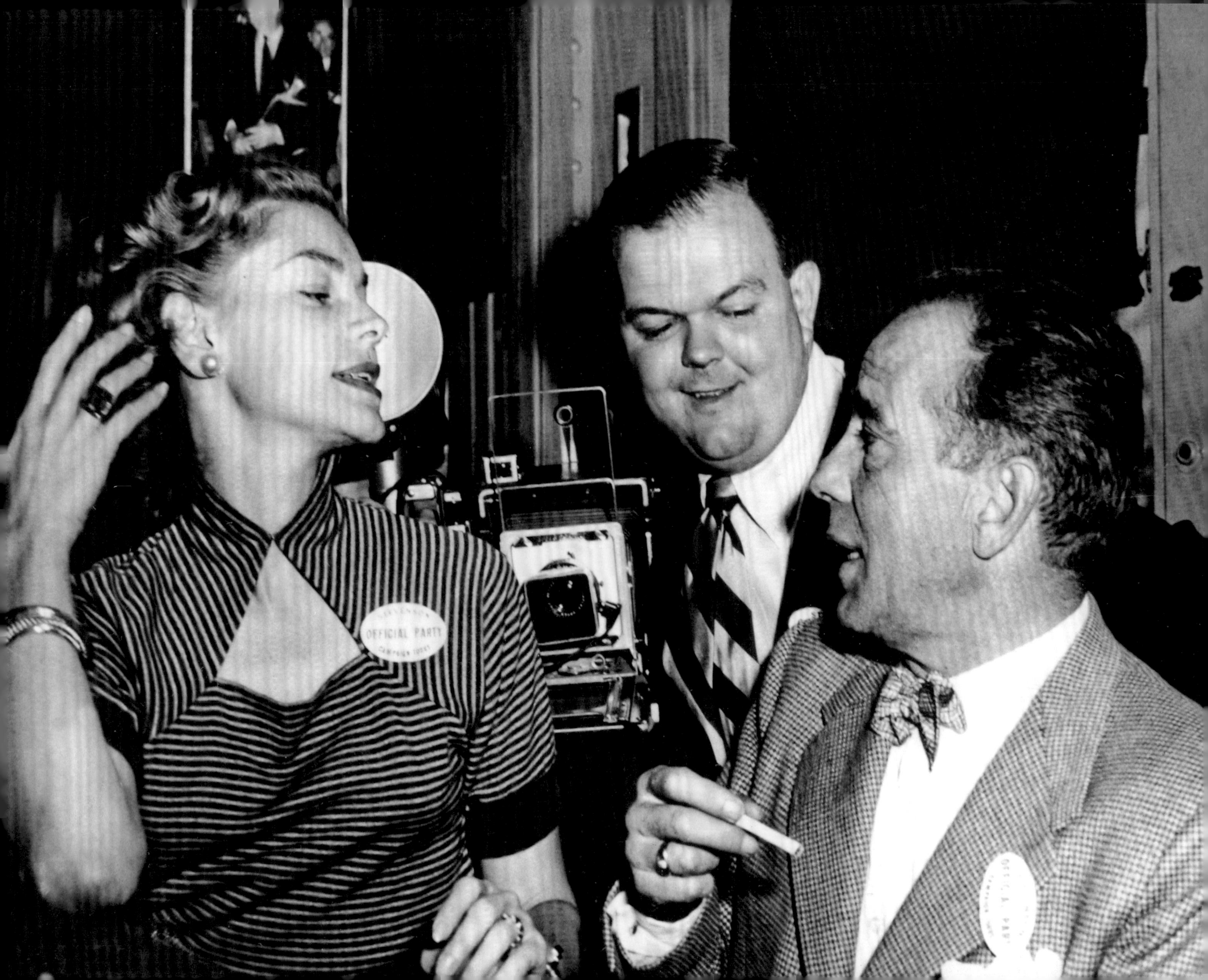
OFFICIAL PARTY

ABOVE: Homeowners on the Hill in the Harris subdivision in 1950. *Courtesy T.E. Finley*

OPPOSITE: Lauren Bacall, left, William D. Calvin, center, and Humphrey Bogart, right, in Springfield for Adlai Stevenson's presidential campaign. *Courtesy Sangamon Valley Collection, Lincoln Library*

BELOW: Harvard Park Dad's Club Minstrel Show, 1951-1953. Identified in the photo on the far left is Sonya Kaylor. The Harvard Park Dad's Club was built by the dads in the Harvard area and was in existence from the 1930s to the late 1980s. In its heyday, it was a community center, hosting Boy and Girl Scout troops, weddings, and local dances. The H.P. Dad's Club Minstrel Show was an annual event hosted by the Minstrel Men. *Courtesy Dianne Barghouti Hardwick*

ABOVE: The Ruth Fortune Dancers, circa 1950. Identified in no particular order were Betty (last name unknown), Priscilla Mallory Nordain, Betty Brents Douglas, Emma Lee Stewart Conley, Marcella (last name unknown), and Othel Brown West. The little girl in the foreground is Dorothy Logan Foster. *Courtesy Beverly J. Helm-Renfro*

BELOW: Jack Dempsey, world heavyweight champion 1919-1926, gives a bear hug to Walgreen's employee Irene Hughett in the pharmacy department of Walgreen's Drug Store at Fifth and Monroe streets, circa 1950. *Courtesy Yvonne Butcher*

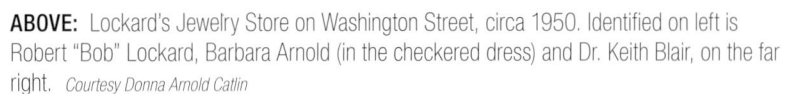

ABOVE: The students of the Westminster Presbyterian Church School, 1950. *Courtesy Westminster Presbyterian Church*

BELOW: Interior of the first "Scotchwash" coin-operated laundromat at 617 North Grand Avenue, mid-1950s. In the photo are co-owners Art Jacob, on left, and Lloyd Inslee. *Courtesy Netsi Jacob Herrman*

ABOVE: Lockard's Jewelry Store on Washington Street, circa 1950. Identified on left is Robert "Bob" Lockard, Barbara Arnold (in the checkered dress) and Dr. Keith Blair, on the far right. *Courtesy Donna Arnold Catlin*

BELOW: Culver Service Station at 101 South Second Street, circa 1951. *Courtesy Sangamon Valley Collection, Lincoln Library*

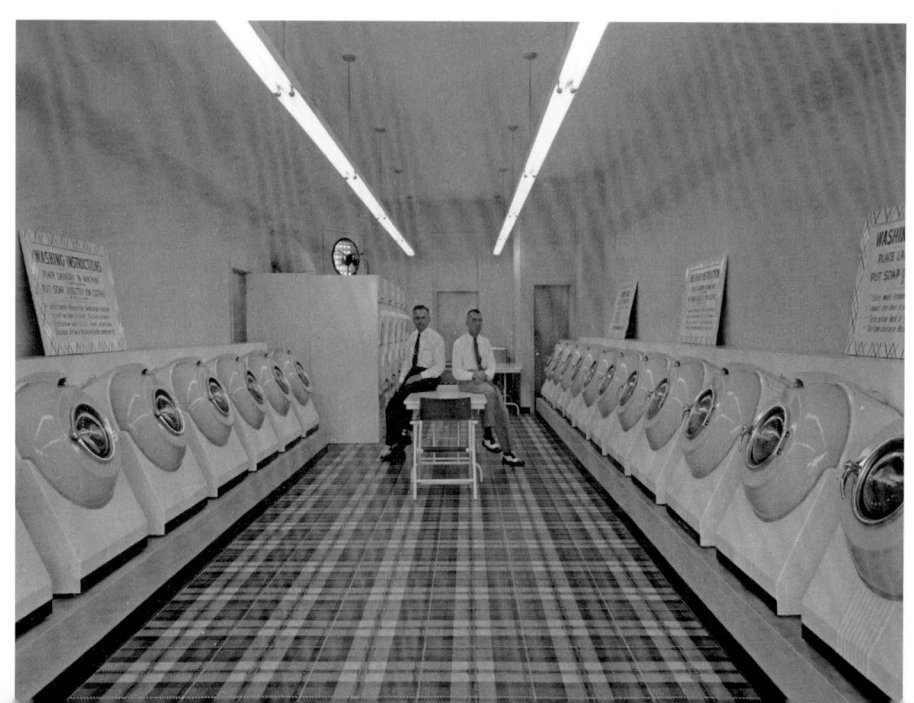

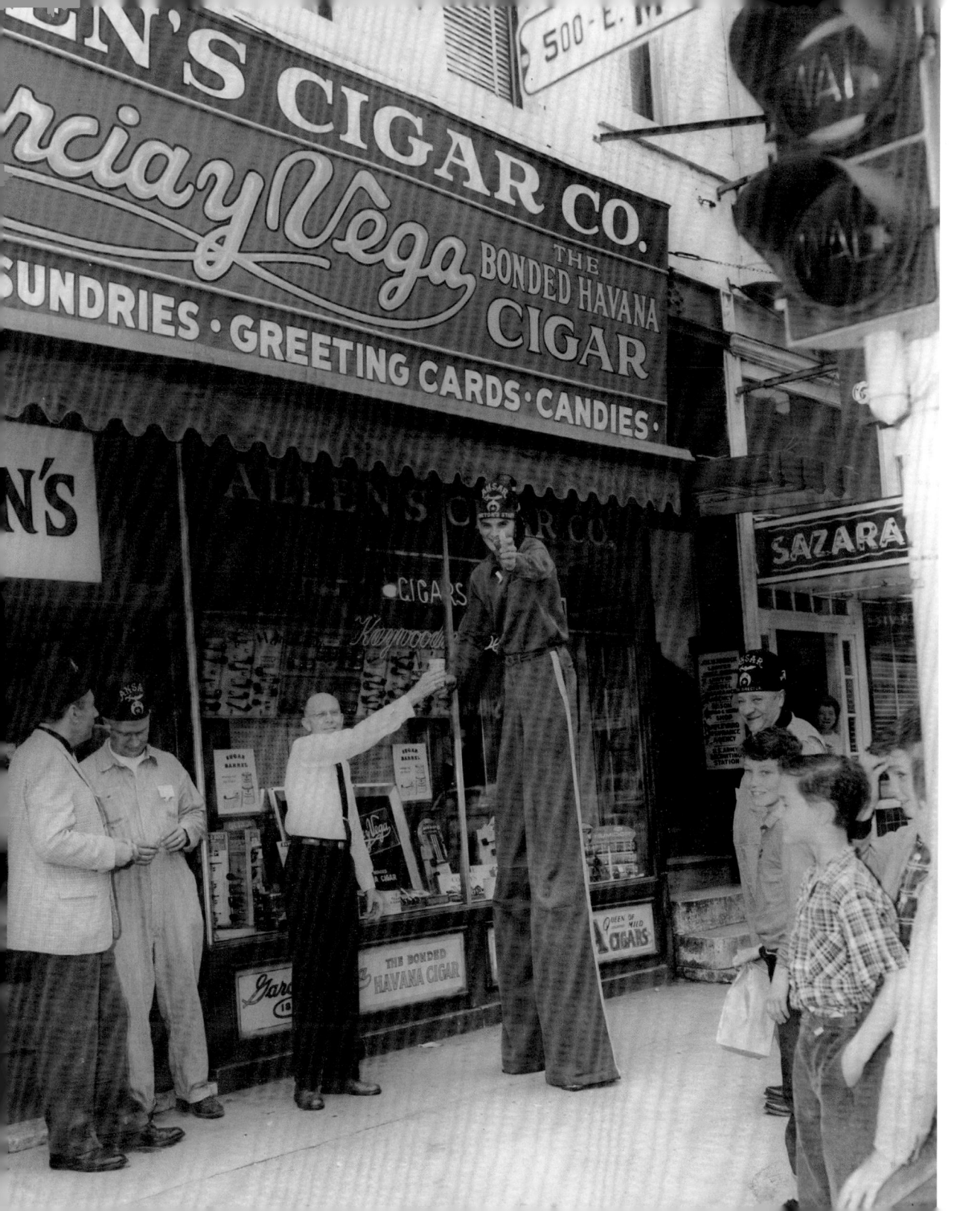

ABOVE: The fleet of Sunshine Laundry at 116 East Jefferson Street, December 1950. *Courtesy Sangamon Valley Collection, Lincoln Library*

TOP: Mr. and Mrs. Anderson behind the counter at Anderson Liquor on 18th Street, circa 1950. *Courtesy Beverly J. Helm-Renfro*

LEFT: Allen's Cigar Co. at Sixth and Monroe streets, 1950s. *Courtesy Bill Broderick*

ABOVE: Carol Sue Wilcoxson Boyce on her uncle Bob's Harley Davidson in the 1900 Block of East Dayton Avenue, 1951. Pillsbury Mills can be seen in the upper right of the photo. *Courtesy Jim Wilcoxson*

LEFT: Women working in the Addressograph department at the State Capitol Building, 1951. In the far back, with her back to the photographer is Bea Jansen, next from left is Bea Young, Loretta Glickert, and seated is Patricia Gager. *Courtesy Donna Griffin*

BELOW: The American Legion Parade, downtown Springfield, 1951. Donald Post (eyes closed in the photo) was Jane Russell's escort. *Courtesy Donald B. Post*

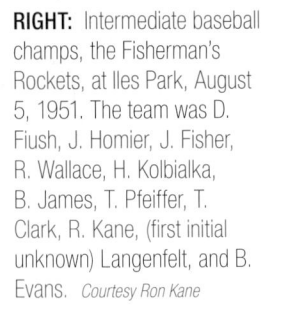

RIGHT: Intermediate baseball champs, the Fisherman's Rockets, at Iles Park, August 5, 1951. The team was D. Fiush, J. Homier, J. Fisher, R. Wallace, H. Kolbialka, B. James, T. Pfeiffer, T. Clark, R. Kane, (first initial unknown) Langenfelt, and B. Evans. *Courtesy Ron Kane*

LEFT: The graduating class of Lincoln Elementary School, June 1951. First row: William Earl, Algimatus Abramitkas, Charles Helms, Daniel Beggs, James Hughes, Richard Miller, Louis Manci, Robert Dorland, Carl Pickett, and Jack Wolf. Second row: Patricia Brammer, Beverly Burt, Allene Doby, Wanda Hyatt, Barbara Braham, Wanda McBride, Marylin Cook, Mary Howard, Mary McGlothlin, Earlene Turner and Delores Brown. Third row: Bernice Montgomery, teacher, Peggy Hill, Carol Foster, Maryann Denham, Mildred Taylor, Barbara Robinson, Donna McCloud, Marjorie Cook, Nadine Meredith, Naomi Jackson, Shirley Timms and G. Wade Elledge, home room teacher. Fourth row: Charles Brandon, Charles Allen, Charles Hunter, Donald Shipp, Gerald Wilson, Ronald Herchy, William McClain, William Edson, Joel Earl, Donald Coontz and Theodore Chambers. Fifth row: Jack Earl, Ronald Spencer, Richard Porter, Lawrence Herchy, Richard Taylor, Aaron Blair, John Burris, John Richie, Jesse Beaumont, Bill Provines, Gerald Harlow and Archie Hendricks, principal. *Courtesy Marjorie and Alvin Krell Jr.*

BOTTOM LEFT: Cathedral Boys High School Variety Show at the Knights of Columbus building on South Sixth Street, 1951. The singer on the microphone is Ken Griffin. *Courtesy Donna Griffin*

BELOW: The Barger family reunion at Lincoln Park, 1951. Russ Barger is front and center standing in front of his mother, Wilma Barger. *Courtesy Russ Barger*

RIGHT: The March of Dimes iron lung is seen in front of the Thrifty Drug Store at Fifth and Monroe Streets in 1952. The two women in the photo are Shirley Smith, right, and Shirley Hughes. *Courtesy Shirley Laurent*

BOTTOM RIGHT: Harness racing at the Illinois State Fair showing a mobile starting gate, August 13, 1952.
Courtesy United States Trotting Association and John Cisma

OPPOSITE: Staff of Public Market, on the corner of Sixth Street and Bryn Mawr, celebrating old fashioned days with bonnets and straw hats, 1952. *Courtesy Donna Bragg*

BELOW: Exterior of the Richman Brothers Co. and Schiff's Shoes on the northeast corner of Fifth and Washington streets, 1952. *Courtesy Sangamon Valley Collection, Lincoln Library*

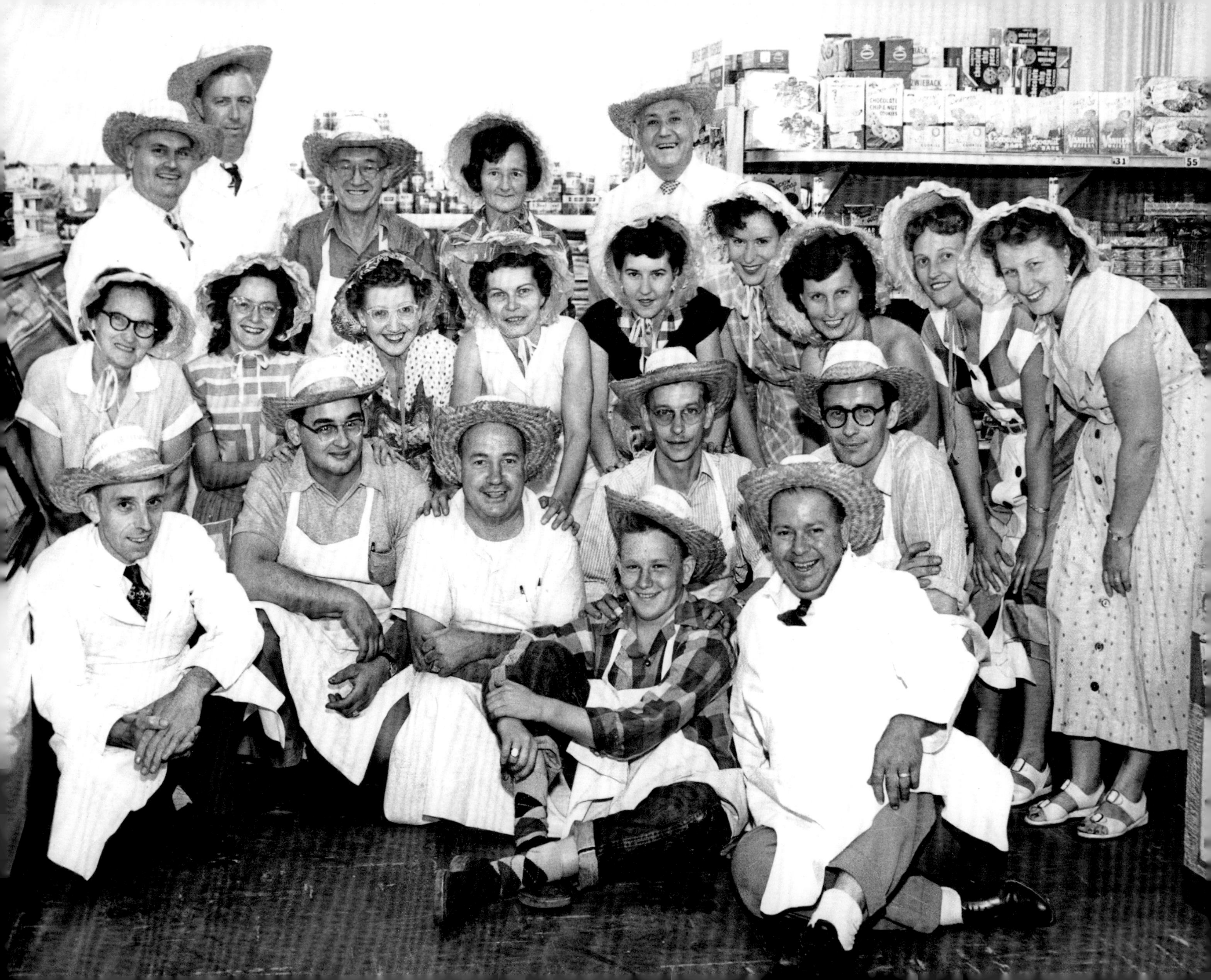
CHOCOLATE
CHIP & NUT
COOKIES
ZWIEBACK
VANILLA
31
55

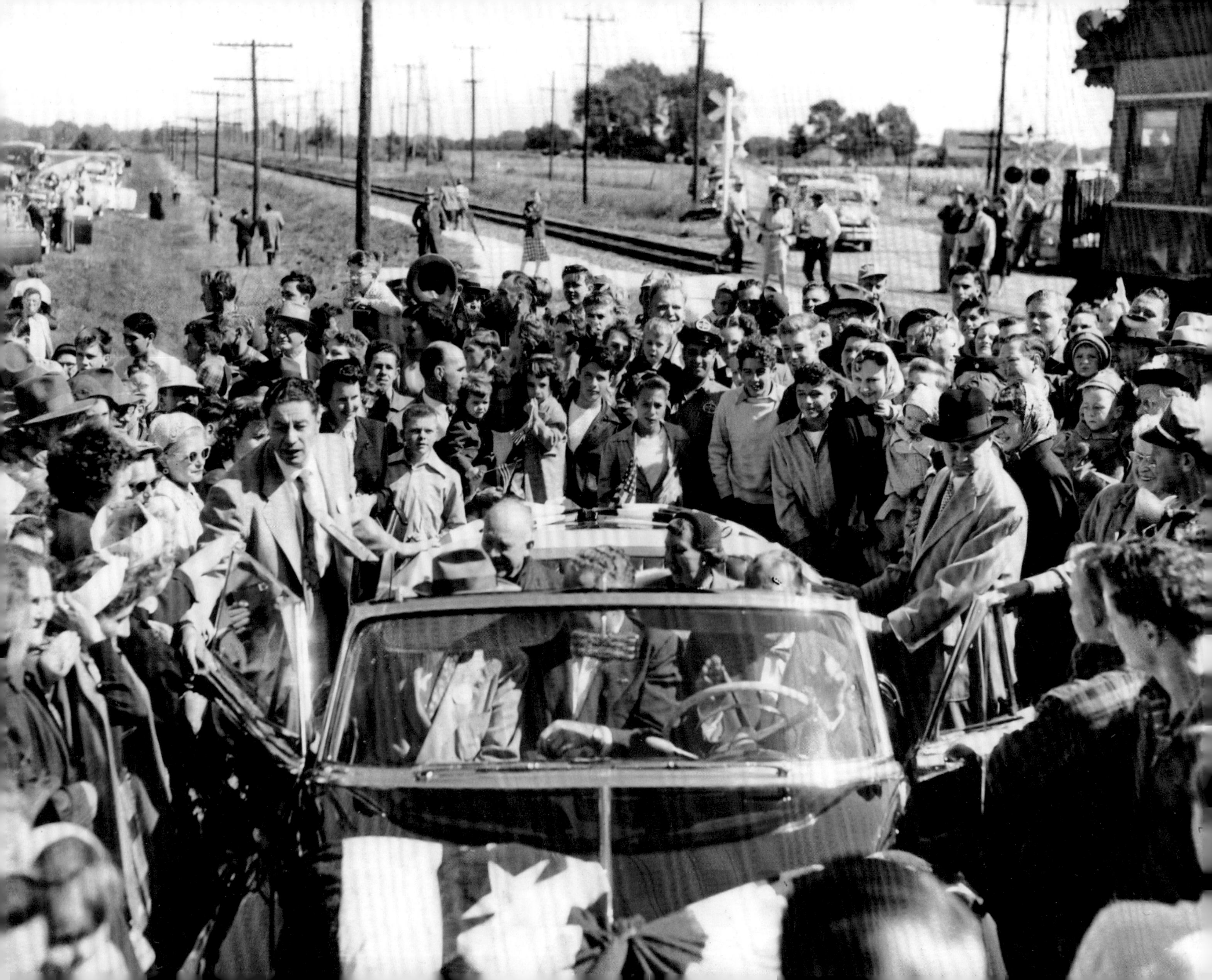

ABOVE: Bob Seaborn, employee of Springfield Transportation Company, stands near his bus in 1953. *Courtesy Sangamon Valley Collection, Lincoln Library*

TOP LEFT: Crowds gather to support local presidential candidate Gov. Adlai Stevenson in 1952. *Courtesy Joe Miller*

LEFT: Mary Jane Masters and Mayor Nelson Howarth at a campaign parade in support of Adlai Stevenson, 1956. *Courtesy Shirley Wilson*

OPPOSITE: Presidential candidate Dwight Eisenhower and Mrs. Eisenhower get a warm welcome from Springfield residents during his visit in 1952. *Courtesy Sangamon Valley Collection, Lincoln Library*

ABOVE: Jim Hoover, left, and David Dalbey at the Illinois State Fair in 1953. *Courtesy David Dalbey*

TOP MIDDLE RIGHT: Dale Hunter with his winning aircraft in a model competition, 1952. After the war, model airplanes became a popular hobby. *Courtesy Carol Brannin*

TOP FAR RIGHT: Susan, Carl Jr. and Carole Ostermeier enjoying a day at the Illinois State Fair, 1952. *Courtesy Susan Ostermeier Tesar*

RIGHT: First and only Jr. King and Queen at the Illinois State Fair, standing with Gov. William G. Stratton, on the left, August 1953. On the far right, is Barbara (Snodgrass) Piiparinen, who was queen of the Illinois State Fair. *Courtesy Barbara R. Piiparinen*

OPPOSITE: Max F. Richter, on the left, shown presenting a new bike to the winner of the Richter & Sons Market bicycle giveaway in 1953. The market was at 501 North Sixth Street. *Courtesy David Richter, Nancy (Richter) Lashbrook and Janet Richter*

19¢
Midget Early June
PEAS
No. 303 Can
23¢
NOW
Stix
SHORTENING
IN
STORE HOURS
HILLS BROS
COFFEE
cheer
cheer
cheer
cheer
Rinso
FREE
MERCURY
This BICYCLE
WILL BE GIVEN AWAY
FREE!
Sat. Apr. 4, 1953

ABOVE: Eighth-grade graduating class from Sacred Heart School, 1953. First row, from left: the Rev. John S. Brockmeier, Donna Carr-Rechner, James Orlandini, Joseph Rock, Fred Grobelnik, Peggy Seitz-Parnell, Theresa Radosevic-Gangitano, Robert Lascody, James Lewis, Larry Ramelow, Donna Chiola-Davis and Sister Mary Cecilia. Second row: Ellen Lepper-Zink, Joseph Krebs, Guy Larson, Jacqueline Misplay-Watkins, Joan Shephard-Eilers, James Hallowell, Kenneth Layendecker, Suzanne Quigley-Pickett, Norma Liner-Jordan, James Finn, John "Jack" Miller and Rita Jannessee-Seiders. Third row: John Baldoni, Barbara Filsak-Williams, Michael Townsend, John Rapps, Judy Nonneman-Hiler, Clara Calandrino-Rogers, Irene Pasowicz-Macleod, Frances Saladino-Eckhoff, Joseph Coniglio, Robert Staber, Irene Butcher-Brahler and Ronald Sexton. Fourth row: Donna Armstead-Fisher, Robert Longen, Charleene Gent-Petrella, Marcia Tomko-Tykal, Leo Evans, Norman Liner, John Whitthorne-Snow, Jean Blackston-Moore, Nancy Zaubi-Cummins, James Moore and Mabel Malone-Martin. *Courtesy Dylan Shomidie*

ABOVE: Hazel Dell School fifth-grade class, 1953-54. First row, from left: Dick Robertson, Tom Palmer, Mark (last name unknown), Rick Broida, Carl Steinkroger and Dick Hinckle. Second row: Toni Ford, Marlynn Myers, Margaret Clowers, Carolyn Underwood, Mary Ellen Schiefinger, Grace Adloff, Mary Culp, Janet Rush, Sara Blauvelt and Donna Thomas. Third row: David Weber, Bill Cornman, unidentified, Kelly Fleming, Tom Frick, unidentified, Jody Willis, Bill Rowland, and Tom Hayes. Fourth row: Pat Brown, David Ewing, Dan Knock, Bob Plohr, Sandy Myers, Cynthia Davison, Ron Caloway, Gail Tate and Mrs. Peterman. *Courtesy Cynthia Olson*

BELOW: Primary class at Westminster Presbyterian Church, 1953. *Courtesy Westminster Presbyterian Church*

ABOVE: Harvey's Tavern and Lunchroom at 1831 South Grand Avenue East, 1953. The tavern was owned and operated by James and Margaret Harvey. James operated the tavern and Margaret operated the lunchroom. *Courtesy Veronica De Rosa*

TOP: St. Joseph School eighth-grade boys' class of 1953. From left, back row: Mike Armstrong, Bob Heisler, Bob O'Neil, Ted Pietzak, Gary Gramlich, Jim Jones, the Rev. Donald Glenn, Bill Bosie, and John Bax. From left, kneeling: Paul O'Connor, Jim Brahler, Carl Fischer, Bryan Dunlevy, Jerry Teater, Charles Arisman, and Dan Cadigan. *Courtesy Dan Cadigan*

ABOVE: Six runners are shown as they get underway for the 50-yard dash at the Illinois State Fair Junior Olympics track and field meet in 1954. They are participating in the finals for the boys 11-years-and-under class. Boys shown, and the positions they finished in are, from left: Larry Meaney, sixth; Mickey Warren, fourth; Larry Milam, fifth; Terry Barton, second; James Leka, third; and Billy Evans of Springfield, first. *Courtesy Sangamon Valley Collection, Lincoln Library*

BELOW: A large get-together at the Lake Club in 1954. Among those known are Bill Stuart, J. Emil Smith, Conrad F. Becker, attorney John Hendricks, James R. Fitzpatrick, S. Phil Hutchinson, Charles Carpentier, Mrs. Earle Searcy, Latham Castle, Sam Coe, Charles A. Boyle, Mrs. James Fitzpatrick, Mrs. Stan Raney, Stan Raney, Carl Amrhein, Buddy Kapp, Judge Stan Thomas, Bob Saner, Betsy Fitzpatrick Burton and Bill Steiger. *Courtesy Sangamon Valley Collection, Lincoln Library*

ABOVE: U.S. Sen. Paul Douglas dances with a supporter at the Illinois State Fair on Democratic Day on August 18, 1954. This photo went on to win first place in spot news in The Associated Press state photo contest for 1954. *Courtesy Sangamon Valley Collection, Lincoln Library*

ABOVE: St. Agnes Parish first communion class on October 31, 1954. *Courtesy Sangamon Valley Collection, Lincoln Library*

LEFT: The Mothersingers Chorus concert given on Sunday, April 25, 1954. The Mothersingers, organized 22 years earlier, was composed of various members of several school PTA groups. In the first row, from left: Juanita Call, Hazel Estill, Bertha Thompson, Nova Plain, Floyd Tompkins (director), Corrine Shipp, Ina Rae Ice, Rose Bond and Eva Fleer. Second row: Enola Slagle, Mary J. Welsh, Mary Roberts, Edith Peterson, Maxine Nolan, Neva Gallant, Marian Howard, Juanita Faeth, Lillian Konrad, Nan Larson and Dora Etter. Third row: Pauline Hinds, Louise Leistner, Eleanor Culbertson, Jacqueline Tibbs, Angeline Xamis, Ruth Townsend, Mary F. Sando, Mary Upton, R. Fehrholz, Christine Bradley and Johanna Meissner. *Courtesy John & Jackie Stites*

RIGHT: The coal train passing by Ridgely Tower, heading north, April 1954. The coal train was pulled by C & IM Locomotive No. 753 and with only one year to run, pulled its last train on October 29, 1955. *Courtesy Hubert Walton*

FAR RIGHT: Ron Kane in his baseball uniform in front of Feitshans High School, 1954. Ron went on to lead many fastball leagues in batting. *Courtesy Ron Kane*

BELOW: Dominic Bianco, Rose Sinitra Termine Bianco, and Jon Bianco behind the counter at Termine's Tavern on Clear Lake Avenue, 1954. *Courtesy Shirley Bianco*

ABOVE: The wedding day of Charles and Marlene Wilson Neal, November 14, 1954. Arlene Wilson Woodrum was her maid of honor. *Courtesy Sandra Colborn*

TOP LEFT: A postcard from the 1950s advertising the wide array of color options offered by the Illinois Bell Telephone Company. *Courtesy Sangamon Valley Collection, Lincoln Library*

BOTTOM LEFT: Judy Lane, Joe Plesch and Marilyn Lane at the Sangamo Electric Co. picnic at the Illinois State Fairgrounds, September 1954. *Courtesy Judy Lane-Reeves*

FAR LEFT: Miss Carylyn Becker, Queen of the Beaux Arts Ball for the Art Association, circa 1955. *Courtesy Sangamon Valley Collection, Lincoln Library*

ABOVE: The 1954-55 Feitshans High School freshman football team. In front row, from left: L. Cardoni, C. Brancato, B. Lewis, F. Marconi, W. Faulkner, J. Gibbins, J. Gardner, J. Gray, R. Smith, B. Volk, J. Stites, R. Hollis, J. LaMotte, R. Bogardus and unidentified. Back row, from left: N. McHenry, F. Gibson, R. Taylor, J. Green, G. Sullivan, H. Shelton, C. Harris, B. Myers, B. Milburn, H. Williams, W. Truax, C. Shepard, J. Carver, M. Webster, B. Meisenbacher, R. Lutes, T. Smith, J. Kelly, D. Yates, T. Foster and D. Tillman. The team was coached by Dean Tillman and assistant coach John McCoy. *Courtesy John & Jackie Stites*

RIGHT: Retirement party for Doc Denton, dark suit, at the Springfield Fire Department, circa 1955. Tom Armstead is seen standing at far left. Joe Patton is fifth from the right, William Vandegrift is third from the right and Bob Denton is second from the right. *Courtesy Sangamon Valley Collection, Lincoln Library*

FAR RIGHT: A guide book to the city and a brief history on Springfield's beloved Abraham Lincoln. This guide book was published in 1955. *Courtesy Sangamon Valley Collection, Lincoln Library*

ABOVE: Mayor Nelson Howarth near City Hall, circa 1955. *Courtesy Sangamon Valley Collection, Lincoln Library*

TOP LEFT: Bishop William O'Connor, circa 1955. *Courtesy Sangamon Valley Collection, Lincoln Library*

LEFT: Lakeside Power Plant, circa 1955. *Courtesy Sangamon Valley Collection, Lincoln Library*

BELOW: Springfield Mattress Co. on North MacArthur Boulevard, June 1955. *Courtesy Sangamon Valley Collection, Lincoln Library*

ABOVE: Ed Poole in the projection room at WICS-TV station in the 1950s. *Courtesy Sangamon Valley Collection, Lincoln Library*

RIGHT: Filming of a political show at the WICS-TV station in the 1950s. *Courtesy Sangamon Valley Collection, Lincoln Library*

BOTTOM RIGHT: Frank Martin, weathercaster for WICS-TV, circa 1955. *Courtesy Sangamon Valley Collection, Lincoln Library*

BELOW: A close-up of the products advertised by WICS-TV in the 1950s. *Courtesy Sangamon Valley Collection, Lincoln Library*

ABOVE: Julia Craig at the filming of a cooking show at the WICS-TV station in the 1950s. *Courtesy Sangamon Valley Collection, Lincoln Library*

LEFT: WICS-TV clown show, circa 1955. *Courtesy Sangamon Valley Collection, Lincoln Library*

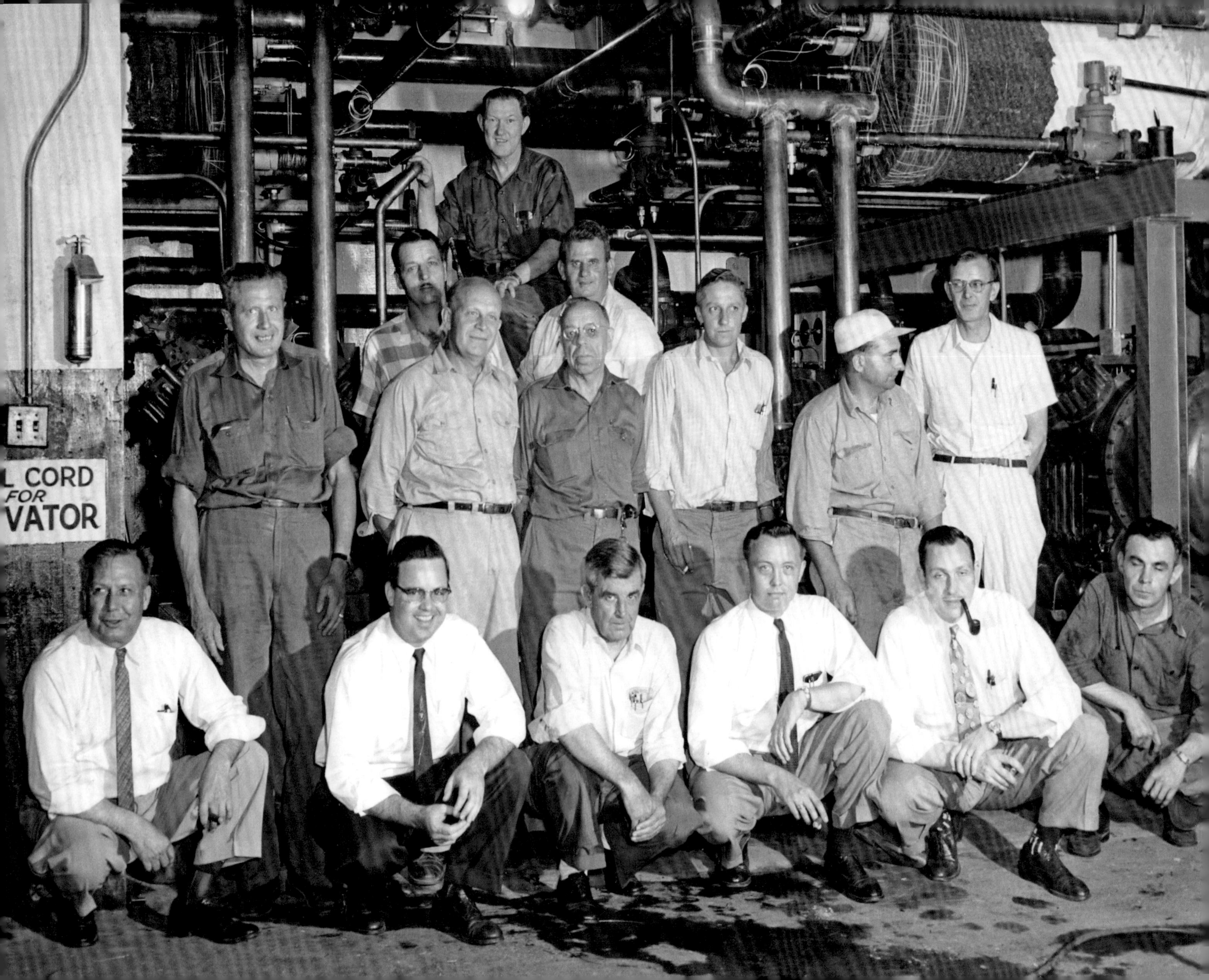
L CORD
FOR
VATOR

ABOVE: Arrival of a new Allis-Chalmers gleaner combine at the Krell Farm Supply Company at 2401 North 31st Street, circa 1955. *Courtesy Marjorie and Alvin Krell Jr.*

TOP LEFT: Brownie Troop No. 147 at Hay-Edwards Grade School in 1955. Seated in front are Mary Farber, Margaret Watt, Leslie Campbell, Linda Ecklund, Linda Campbell, Janet McCurley, Chris Boardman and Gloria Seebach. Standing in back are Karen Salzman, Margaret Hodge, Karen Baughn, Penny Woods, Mrs. Campbell, Shirley Wilson, Lorelei Patey, Grace Sunley, Marianne McClain, Sara Jean Hyde, and Suzanne Hewitt. *Courtesy Karen Sutton*

LEFT: Storefront of Coe's Book Store in the Ferguson building on the southwest corner of Sixth and Monroe streets, November 15, 1955. Coe's was established in Springfield by brothers Louis and Harry Coe in 1897. The subsequent owners were J. Glenn McFarland and Glen Rogers. *Courtesy Glen Rogers*

OPPOSITE: Employees and crew gather in the basement of the Illinois Building at Sixth and Adams streets in 1955. This was taken at the time air-conditioning was first installed in the building. Kendall Baldwin is seen standing to the left in the second row. *Courtesy Carolyn Quinlan*

ABOVE: The Executive Mansion, 1950s. *Courtesy Joe Seiz*

TOP RIGHT: A photo of the Zanders family, entering through the main gate of the Illinois State Fair, that appeared on the front page of the Springfield newspaper in 1955. They always went to the fair on Veterans Day because Joseph Zanders was a U.S. Navy veteran. On left is Marilyn Zanders, age 12; Eileen Zanders Morris; Elora Zanders; and Joseph Zanders. *Courtesy Eileen Morris*

BOTTOM RIGHT: Secretary of State Charles Carpentier accepting an edible license plate cake showing his No. 3 license, 1955. The cake was presented by Charles Midden, representative of Springfield Local No. 147 Bakery and Confectionery Workers Union. On left is George Zellman of Decatur, chairman of the Union State Council. *Courtesy Donna Griffin*

LEFT: Karen Fulgenzi, on left, and Margaret Fulgenzi in their matching dresses at the Sangamo Electric Co. picnic held at the Illinois State Fairgrounds, September 10, 1955. *Courtesy Margaret Sauer and Karen Brooks*

BELOW: Springfield High School Junior Prom Court at the Elks Club on South Sixth Street, 1955. From left are Carolyn Jenot, Donna Morris, Kathleen McFadden, who was Queen, Judy Zimmerman, and Vivian Shofner. *Courtesy Donna Morris*

LEFT: Members of the Springfield Ceramics and Crafts Club at their studio, using a kiln to fire copper enamel pieces, circa 1955. *Courtesy Susanne Wall*

ABOVE: A major fire that burned several businesses, including Grant Store, seen here, on Fifth Street, 1955. *Courtesy Joe Miller*

RIGHT: New switch gear addition at Lakeside Power Plant in 1956. *Courtesy Sangamon Valley Collection, Lincoln Library*

BELOW: Assistant Fire Chief William Vandagrift examines the damage after a fire, circa 1956. *Courtesy Sangamon Valley Collection, Lincoln Library*

ABOVE: The members of the sixth annual Fairway Golf Club Tournament, 1955. Members were Mr. Otha Anderson, Mrs. Juanita Barton, Mr. Donald Barton, Mrs. Mongolia Bradley, Mr. Albert Boyd, Mr. Edgar Bish, Mr. Craven Buchanon, Mr. Kermit Conley, Mr. Fred Copeland, Mr. Lyle Dabney, Mr. Fred L. Harris, Mr. George Hamner, Mrs. Charley Hamner, Mr. Henry Hack, Mrs. Alice Hack, Mr. Enos Hardy, Mrs. Gladys Hardy, Mr. Fred Louis Harris, Mrs. Gladys Harris, Mr. Ivan Harper, Mrs. Helen Harper, Mrs. Anna Mae Jackson, Mr. Charles Lockhart, Mr. J. E. Livingston, Miss Harriett Merriweather, Mr. William M. Norvel Jr., Mr. Floyd Pettit Jr., Mr. James Willis Powell, Mr. John Pettiford, Mr. William Scott, Mr. Dempsey Scott, Mr. Jesse Simpkins, Mr. Albert Smith, Miss Rose Singleton, Miss Marjorie Singleton, Mr. Emmett W. Robinson, Mrs. Floyce H. Robinson, Mr. Joel Williams, Mr. Sylvester Woolridge, Mr. Donald Thompson, Mr. Lois Thomas, Mr. Joseph Tatum, Mr. Thomas Tinsley, and Mrs. Carlena Smith. *Courtesy Beverly J. Helm-Renfro*

ABOVE: Former President Harry Truman pays a visit to Springfield to endorse Adlai Stevenson in his run for presidency in 1956. *Courtesy Sangamon Valley Collection, Lincoln Library*

TOP RIGHT: Boy Scouts Government Day at the governor's office, circa 1955. The Scouts took a field trip to the offices for one day and were given a tour by Mayor Nelson Howarth. Tyre Rees is the first Scout in on the right. *Courtesy Tyre Rees*

RIGHT: The Navy preparing Scouts for a ride in the R4D, also known as the C-54, at Capital Airport, circa 1955. *Courtesy Tyre E. Rees*

ABOVE: Ladies choir in the balcony of First United Methodist Church, which was at Fifth Street and Capitol Avenue, November 18, 1956. The director, Aileen Perkins, is in the front row, center. The choir sang for the wedding of Edward and Helen Brooks. *Courtesy Helen Brooks*

TOP LEFT: View of the Leland Hotel on the corner of Sixth Street and Capitol Avenue, 1956. *Courtesy Sangamon Valley Collection, Lincoln Library*

LEFT: Carter Bros. Lumber Co. billboard on Route 66, 1956. A 1927 Model T Ford was used to advertise "Old Time Prices" for Carter Bros. Lumber Co. during the '50s and '60s. The picture was used on a calendar distributed at Christmas each year. *Courtesy Cheryl Carter Downs*

ABOVE: Cynthia R. Davison all dressed up for a Rainbow Girls meeting, standing by the new family car, 80 East Hazel Dell, 1956. *Courtesy Cynthia Olson*

LEFT: Elks Club dance on South Sixth Street in 1956. From left are Melba Kiska, Clarence Cravens, Bill Smith, JoAnn Lee, Shirley Hughes and Bob Laurent. *Courtesy Shirley Laurent*

BELOW: Groundbreaking ceremony for Glenwood High School in Chatham, 1956. Identified from right are, Carl Ostermeier, Paul Stout, Walter Luedtke (with shovel), Billy Clark, Mr. Morrison (third from left) and Warren Moyer (fifth from left). All but Mr. Morrison were school board members. *Courtesy Susan Ostermeier Tesar*

BELOW: Glen and Betty Rogers at the Prevue Lounge in the 400 block of East Jefferson Street in January 1956. Glen was the owner of Coe's Book Store. He sold the store to Haines and Essick Co. of Decatur in 1973. *Courtesy Glen Rogers*

LEFT: Secretary of State Charles Capentier with his granddaughter, Susan Jane, looking at the 1956 car license plate. *Courtesy Donna Griffin*

FAR LEFT: Mike Gerula in front of the Lazy Lou Tavern that was owned by his parents, Mike and Mary Gerula, 1956. The tavern has been owned by the family for 60 years. *Courtesy Betty Gerula*

BOTTOM LEFT: Dr. Edward Ziegler, left, and Bob Nelch laying the stone work for the tower at Westminster Presbyterian Church, 1956. *Courtesy Westiminster Presbyterian Church*

BELOW: Three residents of St. Joseph's Home take tea in the front parlor, 1956. *Courtesy St. Joseph's Home and Terri Hempstead*

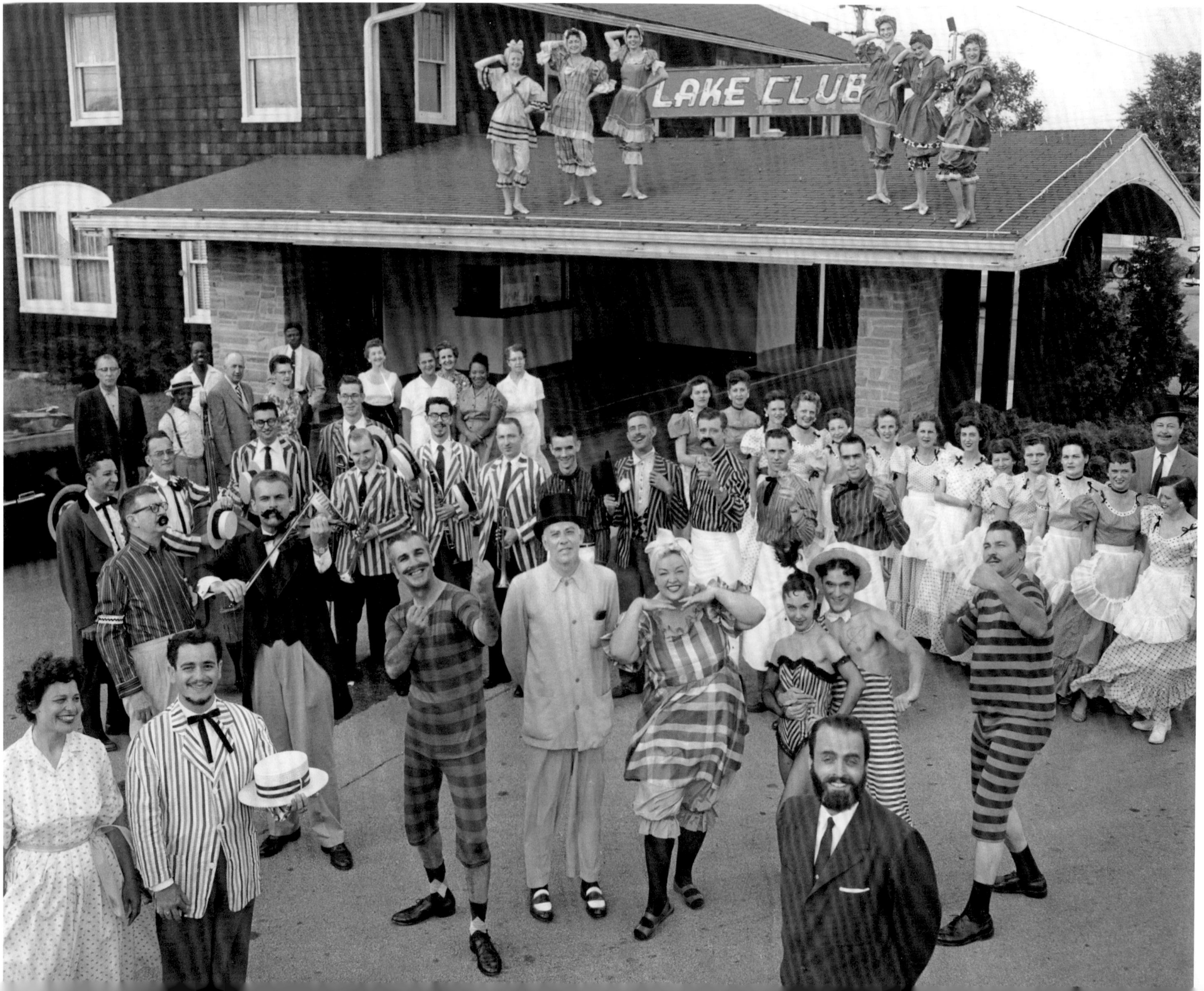
LAKE CLUB

ABOVE: In an attempt to bring in business, the Miriam Sage Dancers rode around in this convertible to promote the show held at the Lake Club, circa 1956. *Courtesy Sangamon Valley Collection, Lincoln Library*

TOP LEFT: Bressmer's Department Store "Style Show" in 1957. The models wore outfits identical to the dolls. In front row are Karen Salzman, Linda Ecklund, Deborah Contrall, Jean Hyde and Janet Lindsley. Standing in back are Linda Campbell, Linda Folkerts, Rhonda Rhodes, Peggy Herter, Mary Ellen Tallman, Susan Bush and Ellen Granoski. *Courtesy Karen Sutton*

BOTTOM LEFT: Soap Box Derby contestant, Ed Wicks, in his car atop the Meadows Gold Dairy Truck for the parade, going north between Jackson Street and Capitol Avenue on south Fourth Street, 1956. *Courtesy Kay Loveless*

FAR BOTTOM LEFT: Frank Moriconi football photo for Feitshans High School, circa 1957. *Courtesy Dylan Shomidie*

OPPOSITE: The Lake Club on July 6, 1957. Owners were Hugo Giovagnoli and Harold Henderson along with employees dressed in costume during the week of the Capitennial festivities. *Courtesy David Lee Jones and Kay Loveless*

ABOVE: Harold and Diane Payne with a young neighbor, in front of a house after it was hit by a tornado on June 14-15, 1957. *Courtesy Harold Payne*

TOP: One of the many destroyed homes from a tornado that struck Springfield June 14-15, 1957. *Courtesy Sangamon Valley Collection, Lincoln Library*

RIGHT: Bystanders watch as firefighters battle a fire at the Burton M. Reid, Inc., building at the southeast corner of First and Washington streets, circa 1957. *Courtesy Sangamon Valley Collection, Lincoln Library*

OPPOSITE: Harry Bick inspecting the remains of his garage. He had been out of the city on vacation and returned the day after the tornado struck Springfield on June 14-15, 1957, to find his garage and television antenna destroyed. *Courtesy Sangamon Valley Collection, Lincoln Library*

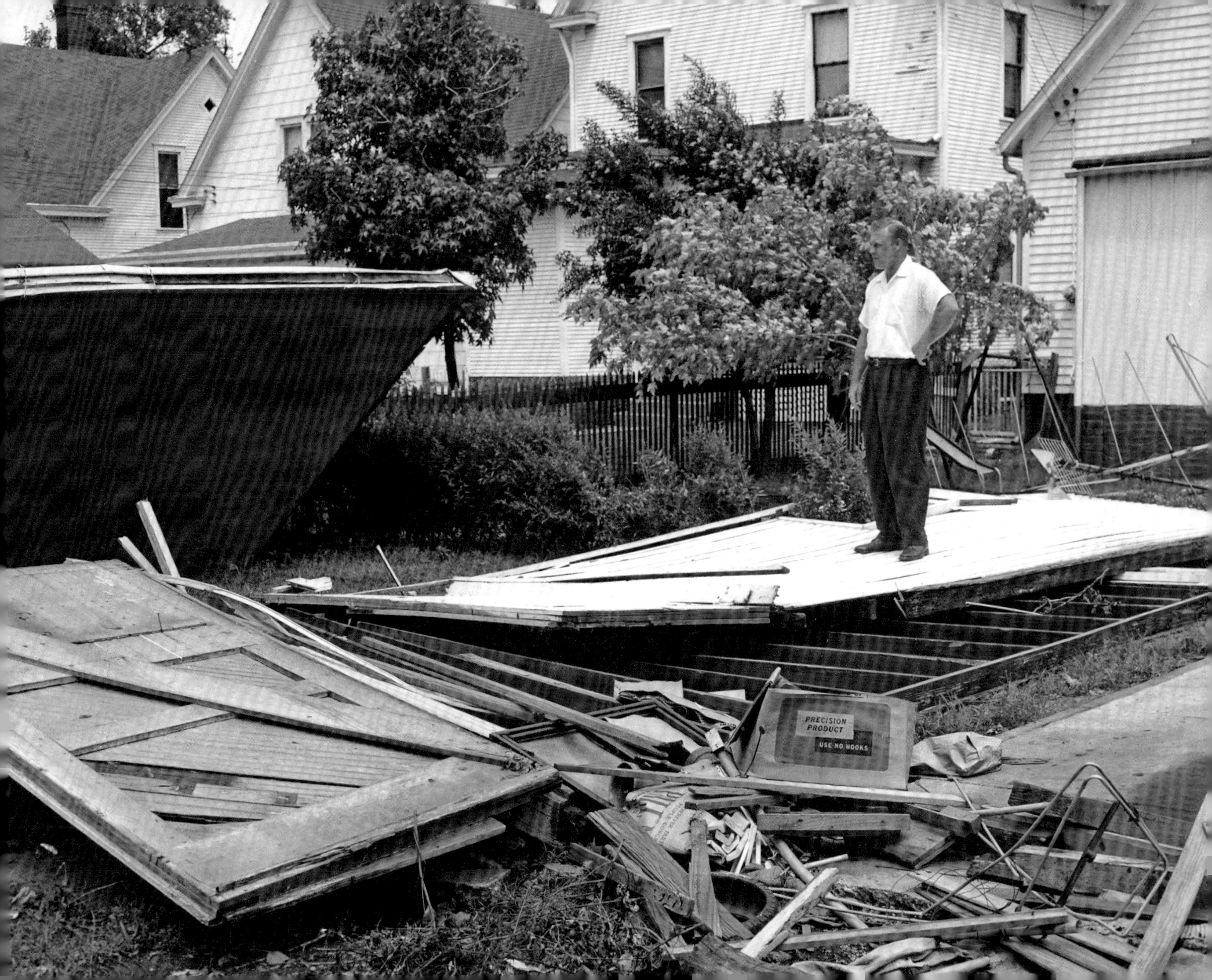
PRECISION
PRODUCT
USE NO HOOKS

ABOVE: Mrs. Archer's morning kindergarten class at Lawrence School, May 1957. At that time, kindergarten was offered at only a few schools. First row: Cindy Embree, unknown, Ken Shoemaker, unknown, Don Settles, Kathy Burke, and Pam Fries. Second row: unknown, Jay Edgecomb, Claire Bogart, Martha McCord, Ned Riseman, and Shirley Frankowiak. Third row: first three unidentified, Janet Franklin, Lynn Hurwitz, Ruth Horney, Henry Dale Smith, and Todd Hirstein. Fourth row: identified are Mona Thompson and Tom Gray. *Courtesy Jay Edgecomb*

TOP RIGHT: A car decorated for the Illinois Capitennial celebration, September 1957. In back is Mary Beth Wander, Al Wander and Mary Wander. In front from left is Frances Loew, Gloria Loew, Diane Loew, Peggy Loew, and Paula Wander. *Courtesy Frances Hendricks Loew*

RIGHT: Caroline Marie Ostermeier celebrating her 90th birthday with her children, 1957. Seated from left are Bertha Ostermeier Uchaez, Caroline Ostermeier and Ruth Ostermeier. Standing from left are Carl Ostermeier Sr., Robert Ostermeier, Delmar Ostermeier, William Ostermeier, and Fred Ostermeier. *Courtesy Susan Ostermeier Tesar*

ABOVE: Kay Wicks Loveless, being introduced as Capitennial Queen before her coronation by Lt. Gov. John W. Chapman, Leland Hotel, June 30, 1957. *Courtesy Kay Loveless*

TOP LEFT: The queen, Kay Wicks Loveless and her Majesty's Court on the Capitennial float along the parade route going north on Sixth Street, in front of what is now the Hoogland Center for the Arts, June 30, 1957. In back from left are Darlene Eddington, Judy Sink, Janie Coombs, Elizabeth Heselton, and Janet Irwin. In front from left are Donna Bridgewater, Joan Wood, Patricia Harvell, Juanita Montgomery, and Shirley Snodgrass. The children were not identified. *Courtesy Kay Loveless*

LEFT: Choir practice in the old coal room at Westminster Presbyterian Church, 1957. *Courtesy Westminster Presbyterian Church*

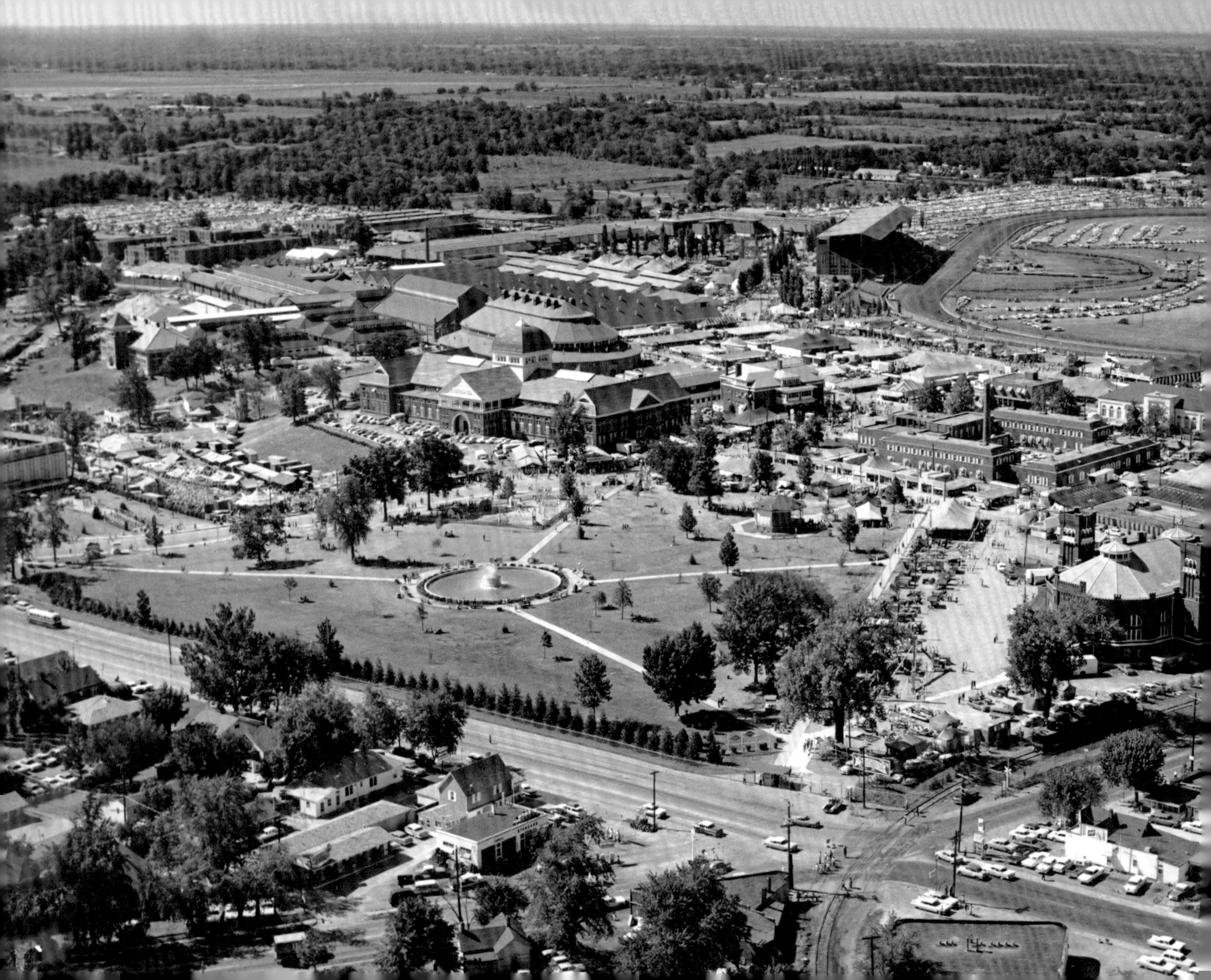

ABOVE: The exterior of the Governor Hotel at 418 East Jefferson Street, August 1958. *Courtesy Sangamon Valley Collection, Lincoln Library*

TOP LEFT: The wedding of Donna Glickert and Kenneth Griffin at Sacred Heart Catholic Church, June 9, 1958. On the left is Louise Skube. In back are Rosemary Aufmuth and Richard Hess. In front, on the right, is Sharon Donaldson and Thomas Skube. *Courtesy Donna Griffin*

BOTTOM LEFT: Cully's Standard Station at 2903 South Sixth Street, 1958. The station was operated by Bob and Ruth Cully. In the background is the first McDonald's in Springfield. *Courtesy Ed Cully*

FAR BOTTOM LEFT: Claire Bogart's all smiles over her seventh birthday Barbie cake, 2249 South College Street, August 1958. The family car, a 1957 Pontiac, can be seen in the garage. *Courtesy Claire Edgecomb*

OPPOSITE: Aerial view of the Illinois State Fairgrounds, circa 1958. *Courtesy Sangamon Valley Collection, Lincoln Library*

ABOVE: Keith Schroeder, Don Cooke, Donald Post, Jon Warhurst, and Danny Ryan in front of the train station on Third Street, getting ready to head out for basic training, 1958. *Courtesy Donald B. Post*

TOP RIGHT: CBS correspondent Dallas Townsend of "News of America" with Carl Ostermeier of Producer's Dairy. Townsend originated his coast-to-coast news broadcast from the WTAX studio on July 19 and 20, 1958. *Courtesy Susan Ostermeier Tesar*

BOTTOM RIGHT: Carl Nolan greets Mamie Van Doren and Hugh O'Brian at the airport as they arrive for the Illinois State Fair in August 1959. *Courtesy Sangamon Valley Collection, Lincoln Library*

BELOW: "Pegwill Pete," aka Bill Wingerter, doing a skit with a chimpanzee for his cartoon program that took place at WICS-TV Studios at the Leland Hotel, 1958. *Courtesy Jack Edgecomb Jr.*

ABOVE: Gov. William G. Stratton greeting John and Jimmy Miller at the Illinois State Fair. Their grandmother, Lizzie Fitzgibbon, is behind them. *Courtesy Joanne Smudde*

TOP LEFT: A CWLP electrical service lineman climbing a power transmission pole, circa 1958. *Courtesy Sangamon Valley Collection, Lincoln Library*

LEFT: View of Fifth and Bryn Mawr streets during the floods in 1958. *Courtesy Dianne Barghouti Hardwick*

ABOVE: U.S. Postal employees named to the newly created Civil Service Establishment Board in December 1959. Seated are Calvin O. Crawford, acting executive secretary; William McElroy, Springfield postmaster; and Wayne F. Williams, assistant executive secretary. Standing are panel members Williams Crim, Richard Kienzler, Albert Coleman, Alfred Urbanckas, Walter Peters and Floyd Brown. *Courtesy Jackie Stites*

OPPOSITE: Abraham Lincoln Sesquicentennial Dinner at the Illinois State Armory on February 12, 1959. Mayor Willy Brandt of Berlin, Germany, was the primary speaker. *Courtesy Sangamon Valley Collection, Lincoln Library*

BELOW: Garden Club members take respite from planning a tea in May 1959. From left are Mrs. Myron K. Lingle, publicity; Mrs. Miles Gray, decorations; Mrs. Milton D. Thompson, program chairman; Miss Irene Garvey, decorations chairman; Mrs. Clay M. Donner, tea chairman; Mrs. Clarence Armstrong, music chairman and Mrs. Sam Lancaster, hostess chairwoman. *Courtesy Sangamon Valley Collection, Lincoln Library*

ABOVE: View facing south on Fifth Street toward Jefferson Street showing the Orpheum Theater, November 1959. *Courtesy Sangamon Valley Collection, Lincoln Library*

TOP: Jimmy Wilcoxson with his father, Harry Wilcoxson, displaying their catch after fishing at Lake Springfield, July 1959. *Courtesy Jim Wilcoxson*

A HOUSE DIVIDED AGAINST ITSELF CANNOT STAND
SEAL OF THE STATE OF ILLINOIS
AUG. 26TH 1818

ABOVE: Carl D. Franke Cleaners Christmas party, 1959. Identified is Stella McIntyre, in the center of the second row. *Courtesy James R. McIntyre Jr.*

TOP RIGHT: Lewis Cormaney, harvesting a watermelon that grew on the roof of Charlie Dodd's house at 1316 North Fourth Street, 1959. *Courtesy Elaine Cormaney*

RIGHT: The Springfield Theatre Guild during its production of "Inherit the Wind," February 14, 1959. The cast was directed by Adelaide O'Brien and assisted by Sara Feuer. The other cast members were Janet Proctor, Harry Troop, Dick White, Robert Cooper, Florence O'Brien, Paul Becker, Richard Pline, Wayne Coady Jr., Dorothy Kuntzman, Pam Nance, Jan Bridges, Martha Bradley, John Bluhm, Helen Babcock, Mandy Collins, Marion R. Lynes, Ted Swinford, Art Rodger, H.O. Croft, Mrs. Earl C. Paulsel, Douglas Kimball, Ruby Evans, Morris Parker, Frank R. Vernor, Emmet F. Pearson, Earl C. Paulsel, Jack Rodger, Adrian Rutherford, Ed Mahoney, Eddie Sotak, Keith C. Vrona, Norman C. Homiller and Hal Crookshank. *Courtesy Dorothy Kuntzman Babich*

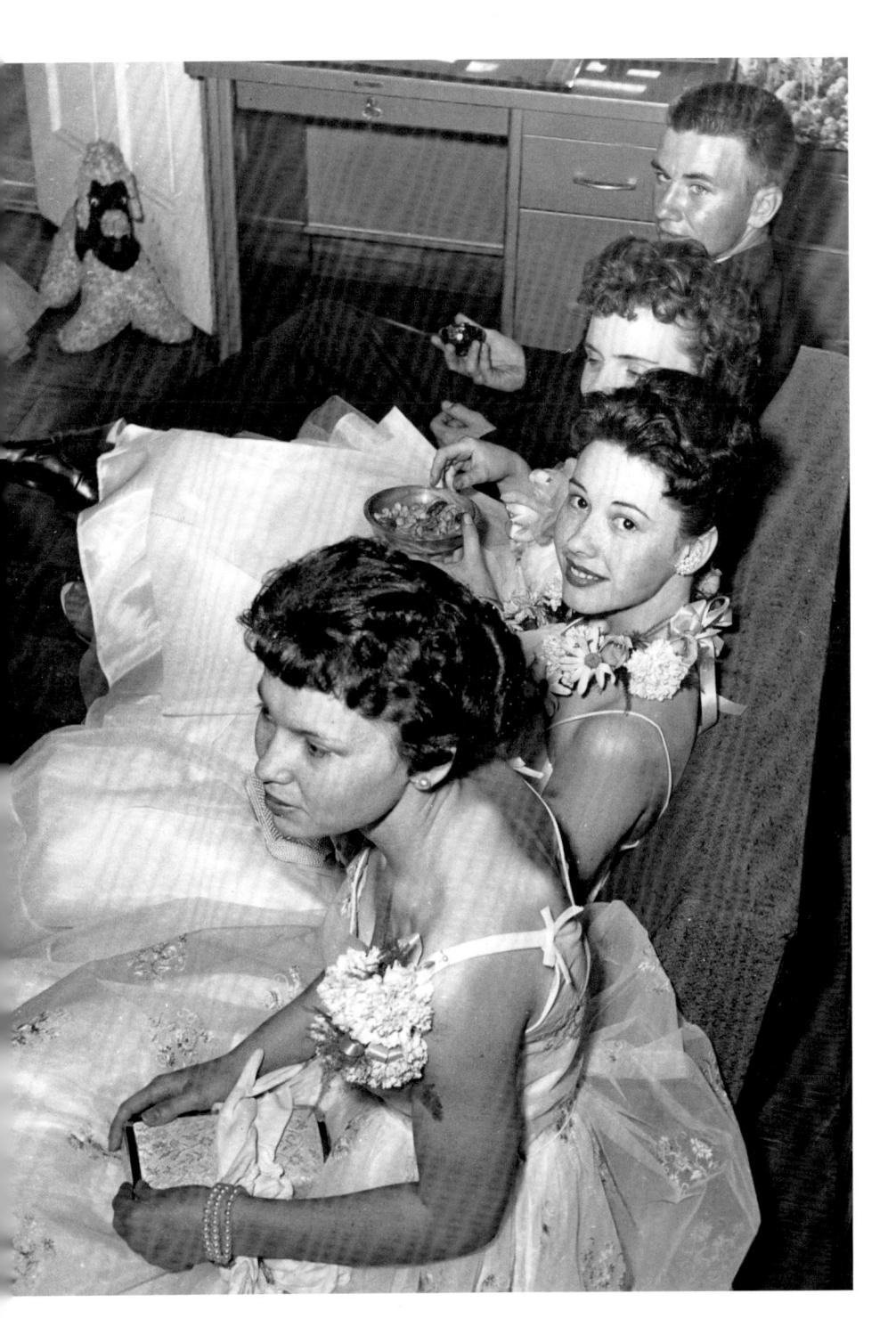

LEFT: A group of men from the Senate Theater preparing movie posters for display, 1959. The man on the left is Ralph Hager, Senate stagehand, who was later killed in an accident when the grandstands at the Illinois State Fairgrounds collapsed. *Courtesy Jay Edgecomb*

FAR LEFT: Sherman High School "Coketail Party" pre-prom party, 1959. Identified in the photo are Sandy Black Grant, Donna Arnold Catlin, Laverne Wilson Leathers, and Daniel "Tony" Leathers. *Courtesy Donna Arnold Catlin*

BELOW: Road Runners Hot Rod Club Car Show at the Illinois State Fairgrounds, 1959. Identified are Joe Mahoney, Harvey Rieck, Larry Rhodes, Paul Lawler, Wayne Harshaw, Don Refine, Dale Johnson, Jim Carmean, and Chuck Bolton. *Courtesy Wilma Refine*

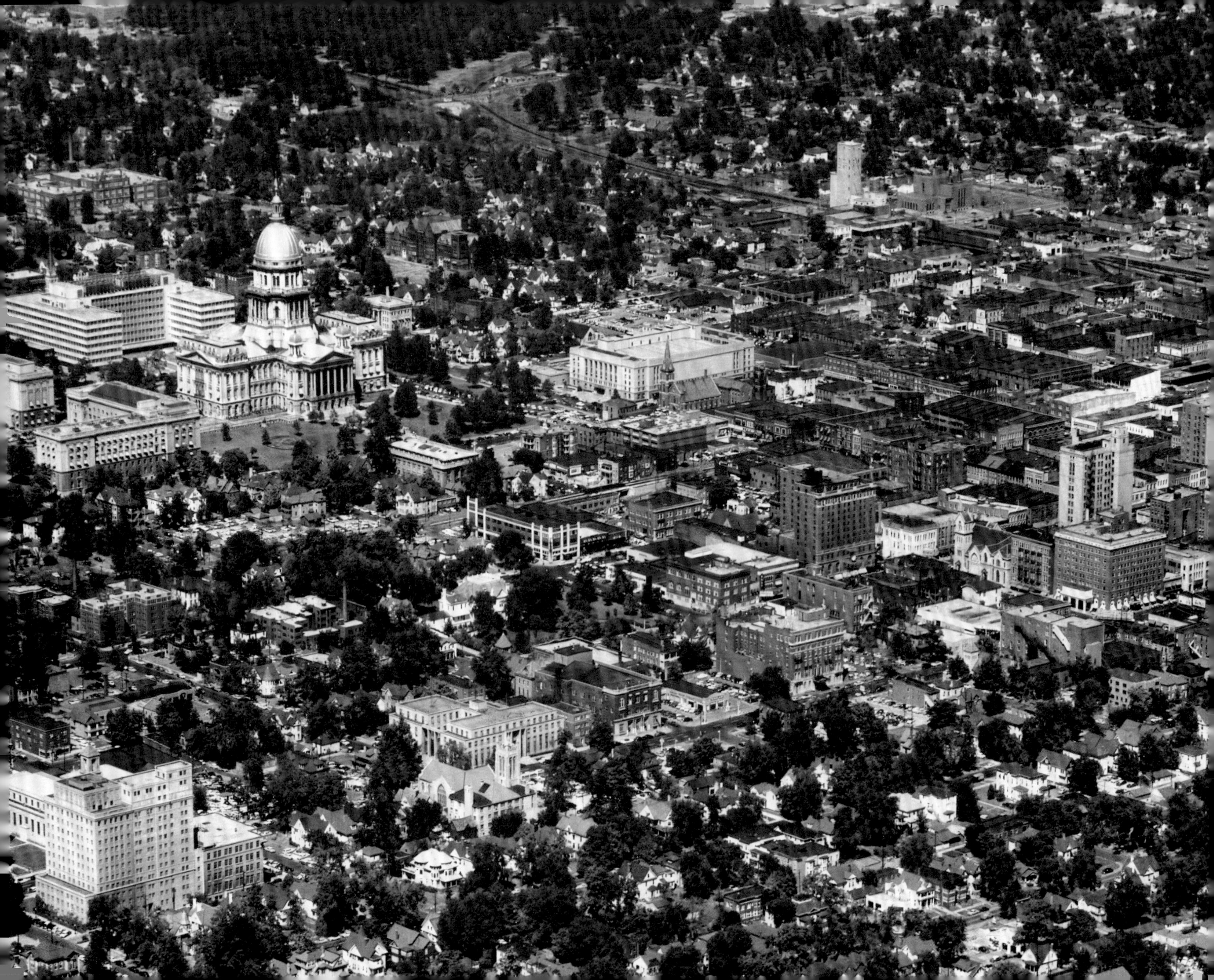

1960s

Some prominent Springfield institutions took on new forms in the 1960s — St. John's Hospital began a period of long-term expansion, while at the same time taking its first steps toward the high-tech heart-care center it has become today. The city got a new city hall and a new Sangamon County Building (though that 1960s structure itself also has been superseded).

The Rees Memorial Carillon was built in Washington Park, and Island Bay Yacht Club got a striking new clubhouse. And in the heart of downtown, the Old State Capitol was torn down and rebuilt as Abraham Lincoln would have known it.

The 1960s are thought of as a decade of protest and youth revolt by many, but Springfield's photographic memory contains only a few hints of that turmoil — visits to the city by Dr. Martin Luther King Jr. and President Lyndon Johnson, and photos of a couple of folk-music groups. The Sting Rays may have played surf rock at a 1964 street dance, but some of the 500 teenagers in that crowd (page 136) probably also are shown in an adjacent photo, begowned and boutonniered, at the 1964 Springfield High Invite.

LEFT: Aerial view of Springfield, Ill., circa 1960.
Courtesy Sangamon Valley Collection, Lincoln Library

RIGHT: Sangamon County Sheriff Hugh Campbell, center, with striped tie, and the sheriff's staff in 1960 in front of the old Sangamon County Jail at Seventh and Jefferson streets. Campbell's wife, Doris, in front in black dress, helped cook meals for jail inmates. *Submitted by Capt. Jack Campbell, Sangamon County Sheriff's Department.*

BOTTOM RIGHT: Members of the Springfield Optimist Club, hosts for the district session of Optimists in the 1960s, are shown at Capital Airport, as they greet W. Arnold Chambers, who came to attend the session. Chambers was chairman of the Optimists Achievement and Awards committee and witnessed the oratorical contest for the district clubs' winners. From left are LeRoy Arvin, General Chairman Howard Fryhoff, W. Arnold Chambers, Ernest A. Ostermeier and C.C. Hoogland, past district governor and civic club organizer. *Courtesy Sangamon Valley Collection, Lincoln Library*

BELOW: The north side of the public square, circa 1960. *Courtesy Sangamon Valley Collection, Lincoln Library*

ABOVE: The new city hall under construction, 1960. *Courtesy Sangamon Valley Collection, Lincoln Library*

BELOW: Eileen Zanders Morris and her mother Elora Zanders in front of the A & P Supermarket on North Fifth Street, 1960s. *Courtesy Eileen Morris*

ABOVE: The Municipal Building decorated for Christmas in the 1960s. *Courtesy Sangamon Valley Collection, Lincoln Library*

BELOW: View of the northwest corner of Fourth and Monroe streets, circa 1960. *Courtesy Sangamon Valley Collection, Lincoln Library*

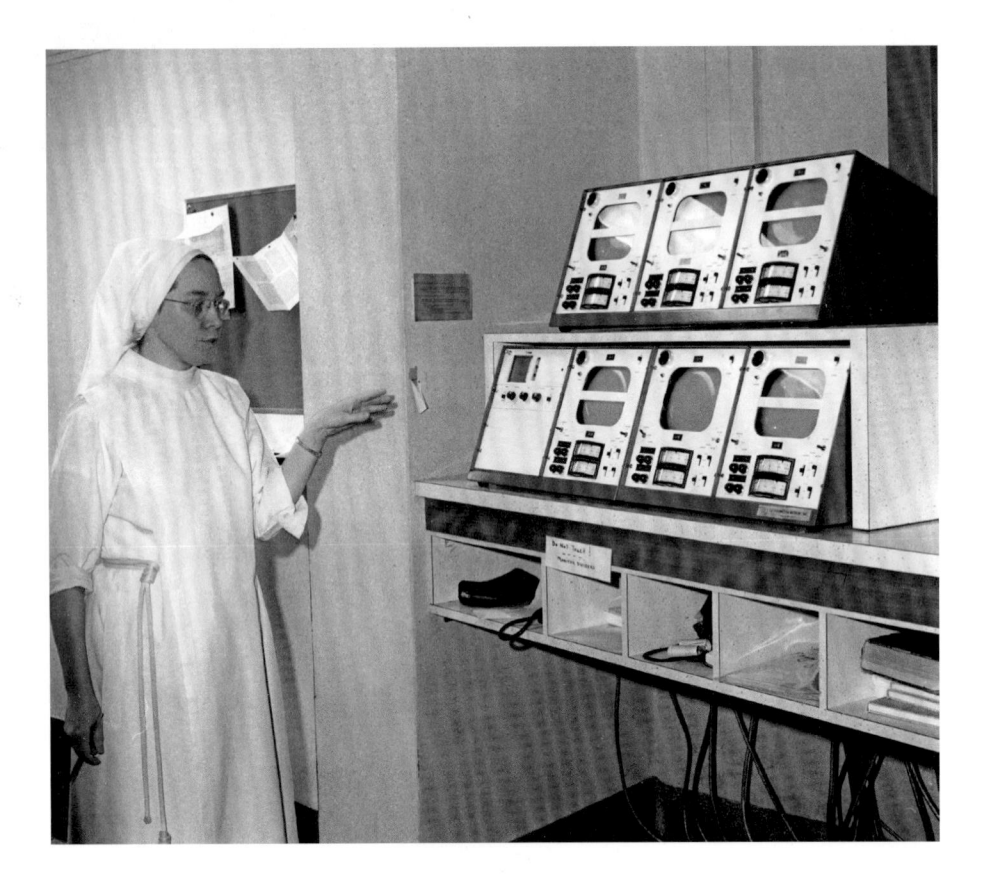

ABOVE: Cardiac monitoring system in the coronary care unit at St. John's Hospital, circa 1960. *Courtesy Sangamon Valley Collection, Lincoln Library*

RIGHT: Daughter of William and Bernice Rogers, Elizabeth Rogers, winner of the 1961 Governor Otto Kerner Prettiest Baby Contest in her itsy bitsy yellow polka dot bikini. *Courtesy Bernice Rogers*

OPPOSITE: Local women from the League of Women Voters cast their ballots, circa 1960. *Courtesy Sangamon Valley Collection, Lincoln Library*

ABOVE: The St. Aloysius Church Girl Scout Troop, circa 1960. *Courtesy Frances Hendricks Loew*

BELOW: The Sweet Adelines gather for a group discussion at the annual regional quartet competition in May 1960. *Courtesy Sangamon Valley Collection, Lincoln Library*

AGUES
thru P
LEAG
Q thru
DON'T BE A
LOCAL YOKEL
BE A
VOCAL LOCAL
VOTE IN LOCAL ELECTIONS
LEAGUE OF WOMEN VOTERS

ABOVE: The trumpet section of the Springfield Symphony, 1960. From left are Joe Bonefeste, Larry Schull, Eurel Hoffman, and Ted Chase. *Courtesy Jean S. Chase*

TOP RIGHT: A group of high school girls, known as "The Findley Girls," performed at various political events supporting U.S. Rep. Paul Findley in the 1960s. From left, back row, are Radene Monroney, Anne Weber and Nancy (Richter) Lashbrook; Vicki Volk is seated in front with the banjo. *Courtesy Nancy Lashbrook*

RIGHT: The "Tenor Band" of the Frankie Leonard Orchestra at the Elks Club on Sixth Street, circa 1960. In back row, from left, are Al Natale, trombone; Ted Chase, trumpet; Leroy Duncan, trumpet; Joe Bommarito, drums; and Jack Frenz, piano. In front row, from left, are Tom Vost, tenor; Frank Natale, tenor; Les Spence, tenor; and Carol Haaker, bass. *Courtesy Jean S. Chase*

OPPOSITE: Aerial view looking south down Sixth Street, circa 1960. *Courtesy Sangamon Valley Collection, Lincoln Library*

121

THE DAIRY BAR
COLD DRINKS
FRESH MILK
BUTTERMILK
CHOCOLATE MILK
CHEESE
MIDWEST ··· DAIRY PRODUCTS
ALL YEAR LONG
MIDWEST

ABOVE: The opening of Homeier's Dairy Fountain, next to the dairy plant and the dairy store, 1960. *Courtesy Maryann Homeier*

BELOW: Members of the Fairview Golf Club, circa 1960. *Courtesy Beverly J. Helm-Renfro*

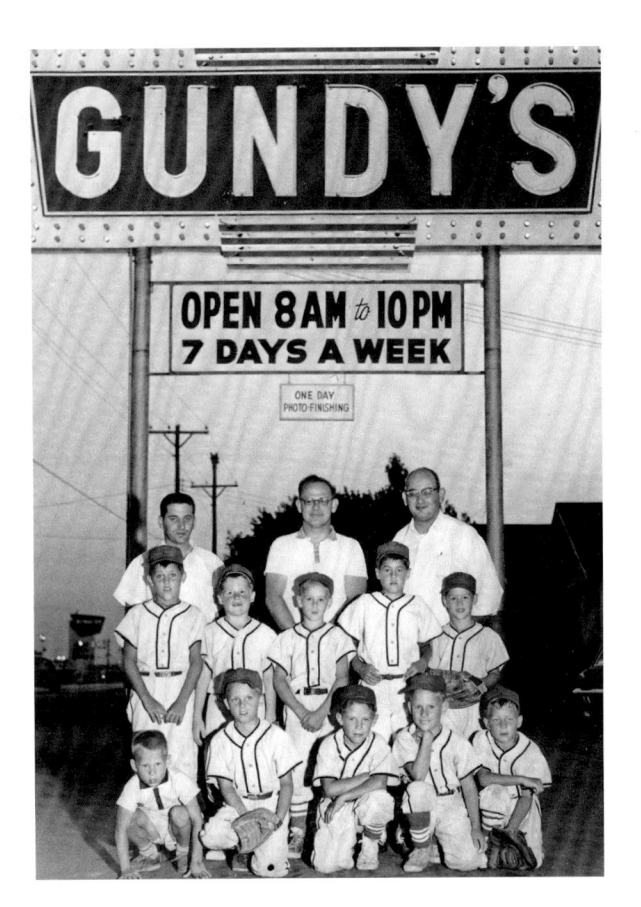

ABOVE: Picture of Jackson Street before it was closed to create the Lincoln Home National Historic Site, August 1960. *Courtesy Judy Crespi*

TOP LEFT: Gundy's Market sponsored baseball team, 1960. Owner, Don Gunderson, back row on the right. *Courtesy Donna Bragg*

BOTTOM LEFT: Joe Zanders in his white meatcutter's coat and hat at the A & P Supermarket on North Fifth Street, circa 1960. He worked at the supermarket for 23 years. *Courtesy Eileen Morris*

OPPOSITE: The "Dairy Maids" of the Dairy Bar at the Illinois State Fairgrounds, August 1960. From left are, Sue Brown, Mary Randolph, Judy Bryant, Susan Curby, Lynn Griffiths, Vickie Faeth, Barbara McAvoy, Judi McDonald, Linda Earles, Nancy Skaggs, Joyce Rollet, Janice Krell, Eva Mae Bancroft, Sue Ostermeier, Nancy McBrian, Anita Bullard, Linda Bullard, Karen Woodcok, Lila Divine and Jan Logan with Mr. M.G. Van Buskirk. In the back are Jim May, Gene Dodsworth, John Harrison, and Gary Riechert. *Courtesy Susan Ostermeier Tesar*

ABOVE: Members of a local baseball team gather for a group photo at Black Hawk Grade School at First and Highland streets, August 1960. Identified is Owen Linden, age 12, in the second row, second in from the right. *Courtesy Joseph Alan Linder*

TOP RIGHT: Introducing a new product at Pillsbury, circa 1960. Fourth in from left is Ernest Philman, who retired after 40 years. *Courtesy Philmon Family*

RIGHT: This photo was taken during the 50th wedding anniversary celebration of William John West and Ella Mae McNally West, circa 1960. William and Ella owned and operated the Aetna Hotel, at Fourth and Jefferson streets, 1942-1962. Back row, from left are sons Harold Dean West, Wayne West and John West. In front are Ella and William West. *Courtesy Phyliss West*

OPPOSITE: Three residents of St. Joseph's Home prepare the birdbath in the front yard, 1960. *Courtesy St. Joseph's Home and Terri Hempstead*

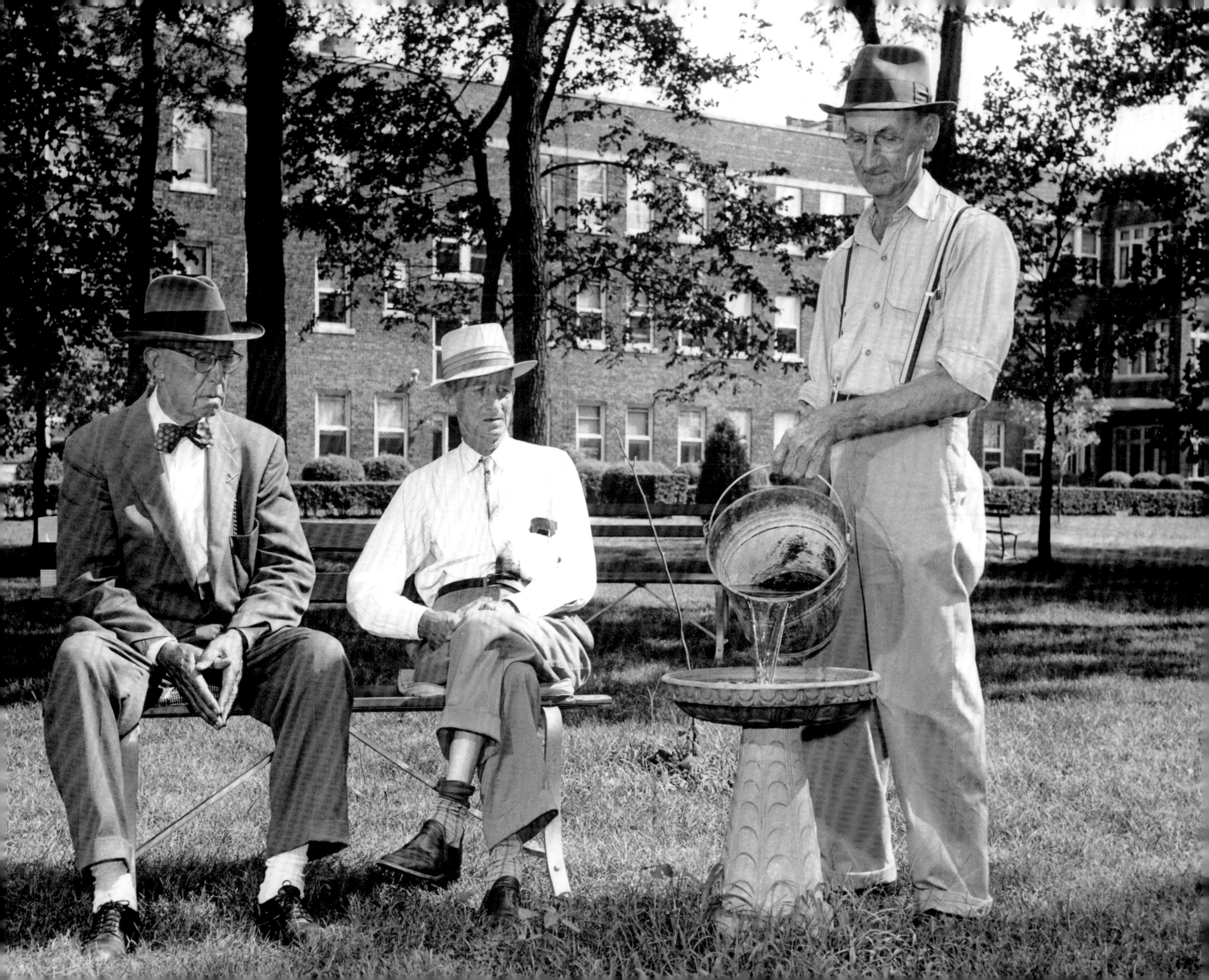

ABOVE: Graduating class of Glenwood High School, Chatham, 1961. This was the first class to attend the high school all four years. In front, from left: Nancy Foster, Jerilee Slaughter, Carole Jean Ostermeier, Patty Lewis, Beverly Bettis, Gregory Wilson, Dick Broaddus, Paulette Liles, Pat Brown, Susie Stebbins, Joyce Conwill and Linda Stevens. Second row: Dick Rentsch, Rosa Atchinson, Martha Foster, Sharon Spicer, Pat Head, Mary Milner, Dale Summers, Bob Krueger, Janet Eldridge, Joann Darlin, Janice Krell, Velma Syson, Marilyn McLean and Alex Jones. Third row: Roy Mitts, Rick Fiersten, Ed Ridgeway, James Dunham, David Ostermeier, Valerie Edwards (Wales), Sue Ostermeier, Helena McKnight, Sue Schweighart, Charles Dudley, Joe Ori, Gary Earles, Ron Cloyd, Jack Beck and Logan McClelland. Fourth row: Tom Mundis, Dick Zillion, Cloyd Hunt, Pete Woody, Gary Mendenhall, Gary Wood, Allan Cornelius, Clavin Anderson, Gene Dodsworth, Jay Philpott, Maurice Busch, Bip Bradley and Niles Nimmo. *Courtesy Susan Ostermeier Tesar*

RIGHT: A City Water, Light and Power crew hard at work, circa 1961. *Courtesy Sangamon Valley Collection, Lincoln Library*

OPPOSITE: The Springfield Municipal Band on the steps of the Centennial Building after a parade, 1962. The director was Homer Mountz, on the far right in front, and the band manager was Jack Wicks, on the far left, in the front row. *Courtesy Jean S. Chase and Sangamon Valley Collection, Lincoln Library*

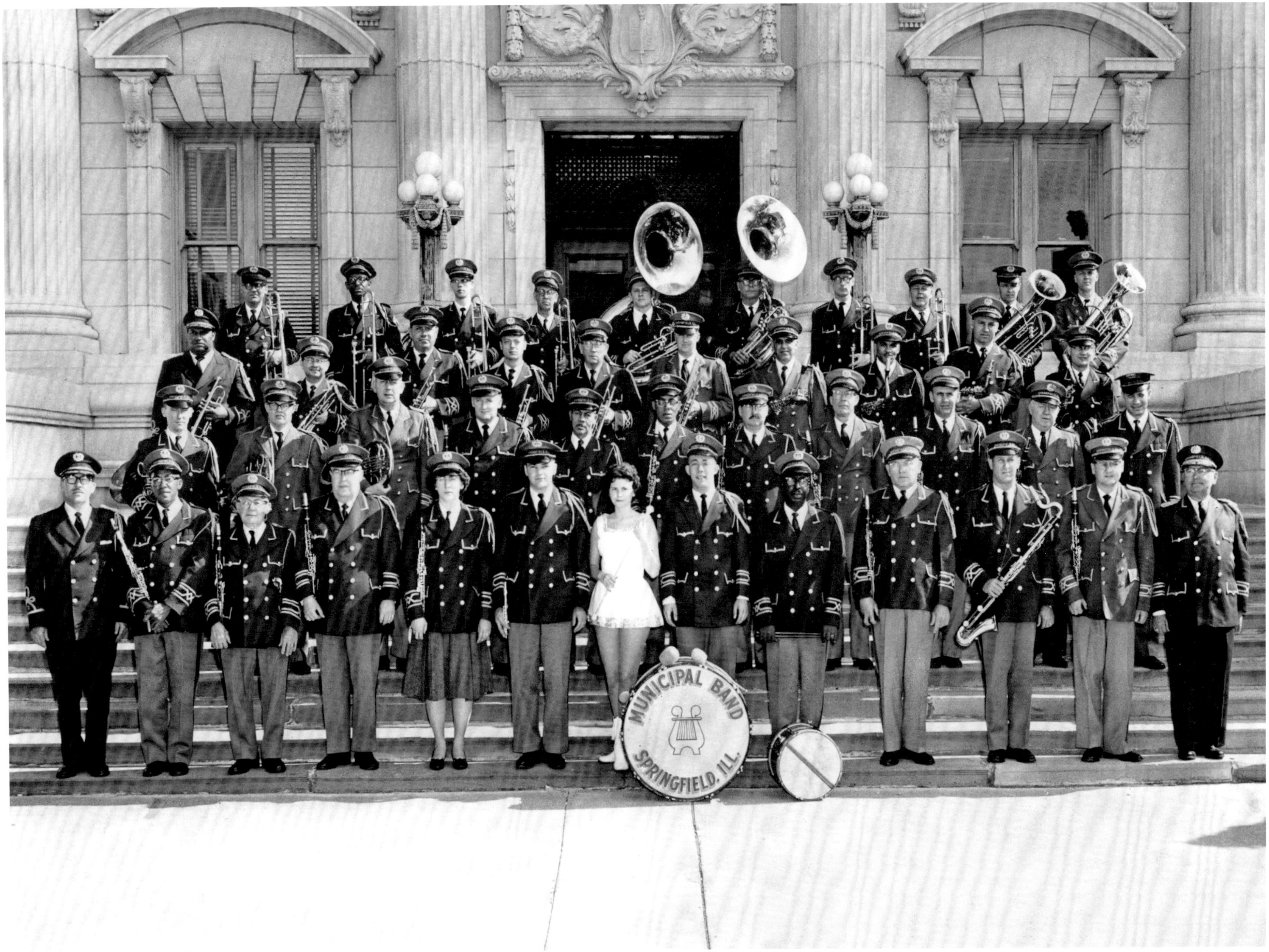
MUNICIPAL BAND
SPRINGFIELD, ILL.

ABOVE: Boys at their campfire during camp day at YMCA Camp Wa-Kon-Tah at Lake Springfield, circa 1960. *Courtesy Jill Steiner*

TOP RIGHT: The Glenwood High School junior/senior prom at the Abraham Lincoln Hotel, 1961. Seated, from left: Susan Burtle, Paula Kay Bridgewater, Barb Sallenger, Linda Vanselow, Patti Lewis, Sue Ostermeier, Jerilee Slaughter, Susie Stebbins, Martha Moyer, Linda Earles, Mary Jean Long, Margaret (Missy) Leahy and Janice Krell. Second row: Jonette White, Martha Foster, Irma Kay Moore, Carole Ostermeier, Nancy Skaggs, Sandy Burton, Valerie Edwards, Sue Schweighart, Ann Aschaur, Linda Wilborn, Ann Lee and Nancy Foster. Third row: Danny Flynn, Gary Marr, Lyle Sharp, Dale Scheafer, Dave Stark, Roy McAfee, Wayne Mendenhall, Niles Nimmo, Richard Haak, Alfred Ostermeier, Carl Mundis, Jerry Mundis and Chuck Kerr. Fourth row: Bernard Armbruster, Pat Sullivan, Bill Schultz, Ed Chorn, Maurice Busch, Joe Ori, Charles Krell, R.B. Young, Pete Woody, Garl Earles, Ron Hohimer and Jim Ashton. *Courtesy Susan Ostermeier Tesar*

BOTTOM RIGHT: The "Big Bosses' Day" of the YMCA past and present bosses, January 31, 1961. In front from left: Domenic "Mesquite" Giachetto, 1951; Carl F. "Rawhide" Ostermeier, 1956; Douglas M. "Deacon" Brown, 1954; Ward M. "Sangamo Sage" Johnson, 1953; Carl H. "Sagebrush" Weber, 1950; Harold D. "Ropin'" Chance, 1952 and Tom F. "Cactus" Paris, 1954. In back row: Rex A. "Piute" Weber, 1958; Clarence R. "Highpockets" Evans, 1957; James P. "Bunk House" Bolinger, 1955; Henry M. "Bar Nuthin'" Lutz, 1949; Bill "Grizzly" Greeley, Jr., 1959; Will "Wild Bill" Wingerter, 1960. Ralph "Big Toe" Blalock, 1946, also participated in the roundup, but could not be present for the photo. Holding the lariat around the group was Big Boss Harold "Cy" Hawkins. *Courtesy Susan Ostermeier Tesar*

LEFT: Bob Volle of Volle Electric Service Co. and a representative from Bell Founders of Holland wire the smallest of the carillon bells in Washington Park, 1961. The smallest bell was 22 pounds. *Courtesy Judy Volle*

BOTTOM LEFT: Pamela Pitchford, age 5; and David Pitchford, age 3; getting their photo taken with Santa at the Myers Brothers Department Store, December 1961. *Courtesy Phyllis Pitchford*

BELOW: Some of the bells arriving at the construction site for the Thomas Rees Memorial Carillon in Washington Park, 1961. *Courtesy Judy Lane-Reeves*

ABOVE: Second birthday celebration at Gundy's Market with celebrity Tex Lee, 1333 Wabash Avenue, 1961. Also identified in the photo was owner Don Gunderson and three of his five daughters, Donna Lea, Kathy Sue and Mary Jane. *Courtesy Donna Bragg*

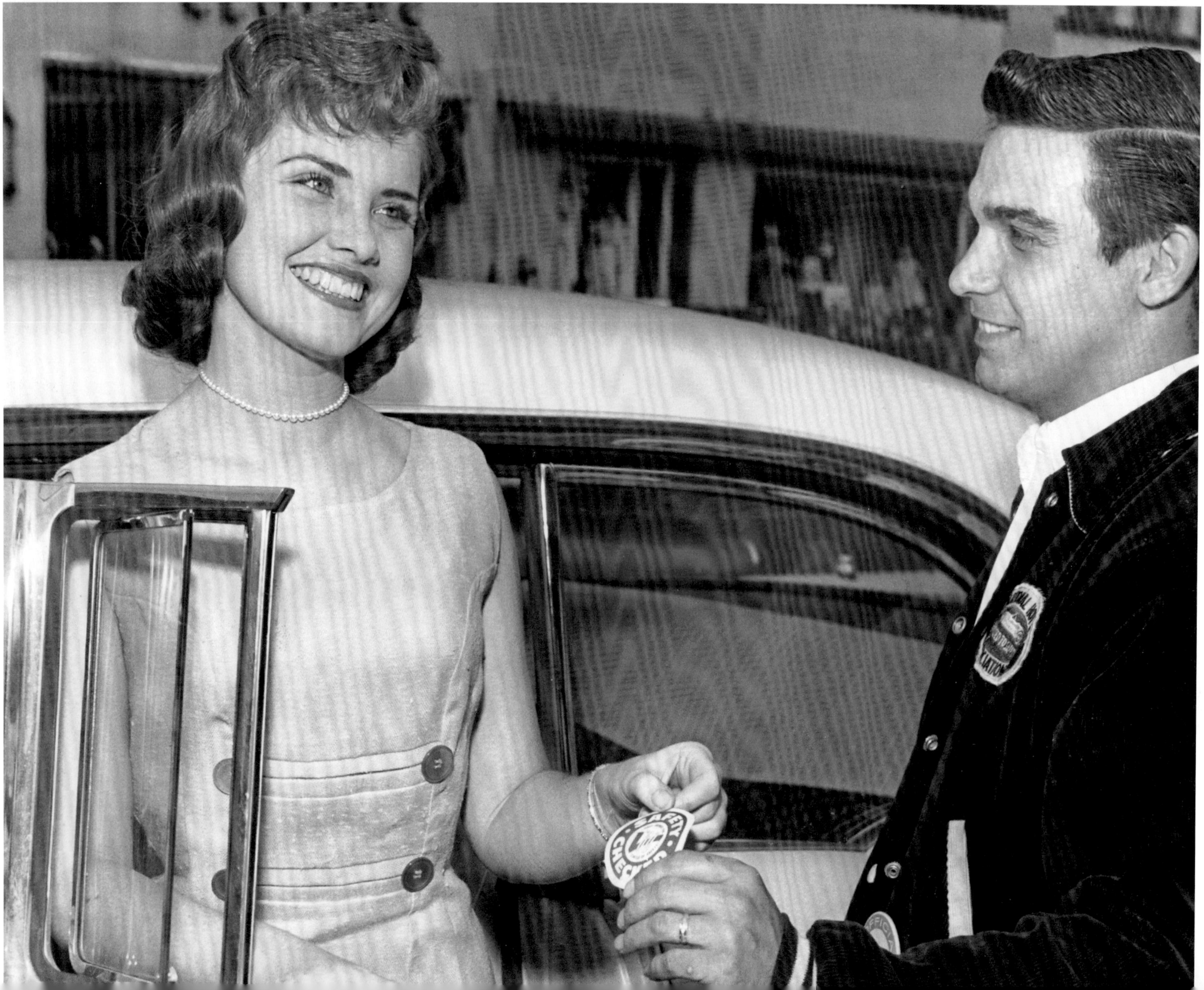
SAFETY

ABOVE: Boys gather to raise the flag before the first period of day-camp at YMCA Camp Wa-Kon-Tah, June 11-17, 1961. *Courtesy Jill Steiner*

OPPOSITE: Road Runners Hot Rod Club "safety check" at Sixth Street, between Adams and Washington streets, 1961. "Miss Springfield" receives the OK from Don Refine. *Courtesy Wilma Refine*

BELOW: The first African-American U.S. House page being appointed since the Civil War, at Zion Church, 1962. Frank Mitchell was appointed by Paul Findley. In the photo from left are Irv Smith, Mrs. Van Baron, Frank Mitchell, and Charles Spencer, president of the NAACP. *Courtesy Irv Smith*

ABOVE: This photo of David Richter, 4 years old, appeared in the Illinois State Journal on Wednesday, October 24, 1962. The photo was taken while David was riding around his neighborhood. He wanted "tickers" on his car, just like his parents, Norman and Eleanor Richter. *Courtesy Nancy (Richter) Lashbrook (sister)*

LEFT: The Thomas Rees Memorial Carillon, Washington Park, 1962. One of the largest and finest carillons in the world, standing 132 feet high and it stands at the highest elevation point in the city of Springfield. *Courtesy Judy Volle*

ABOVE: President John F. Kennedy rides into town from the Springfield airport in the early 1960s. To the right of Kennedy is Sidney Yates, U.S. Senate candidate, and Gov. Otto Kerner. *Courtesy Sangamon Valley Collection, Lincoln Library*

RIGHT: Abraham Lincoln's Tomb in July 1962. *Courtesy Chris Mehuys*

FAR RIGHT: Abraham Lincoln's Home, July 1962. *Courtesy Chris Mehuys*

OPPOSITE: President Kennedy shakes the hand of a Springfield man during his visit in the early 1960s. *Courtesy Sangamon Valley Collection, Lincoln Library*

BELOW: John Glenn's capsule from his sub-orbital flight is on display on what is now the Old Capitol Square, 1962. *Courtesy John Davidson*

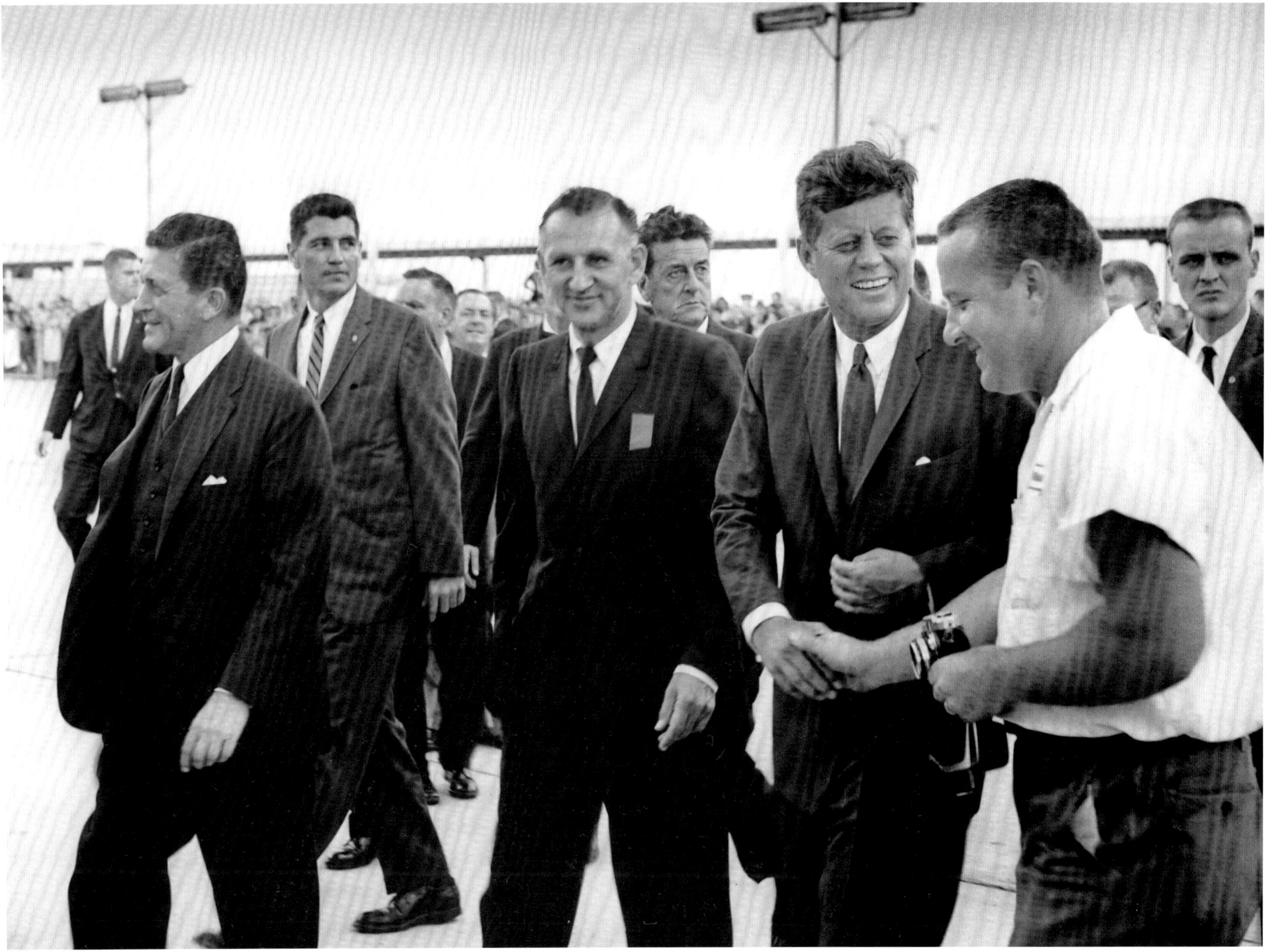

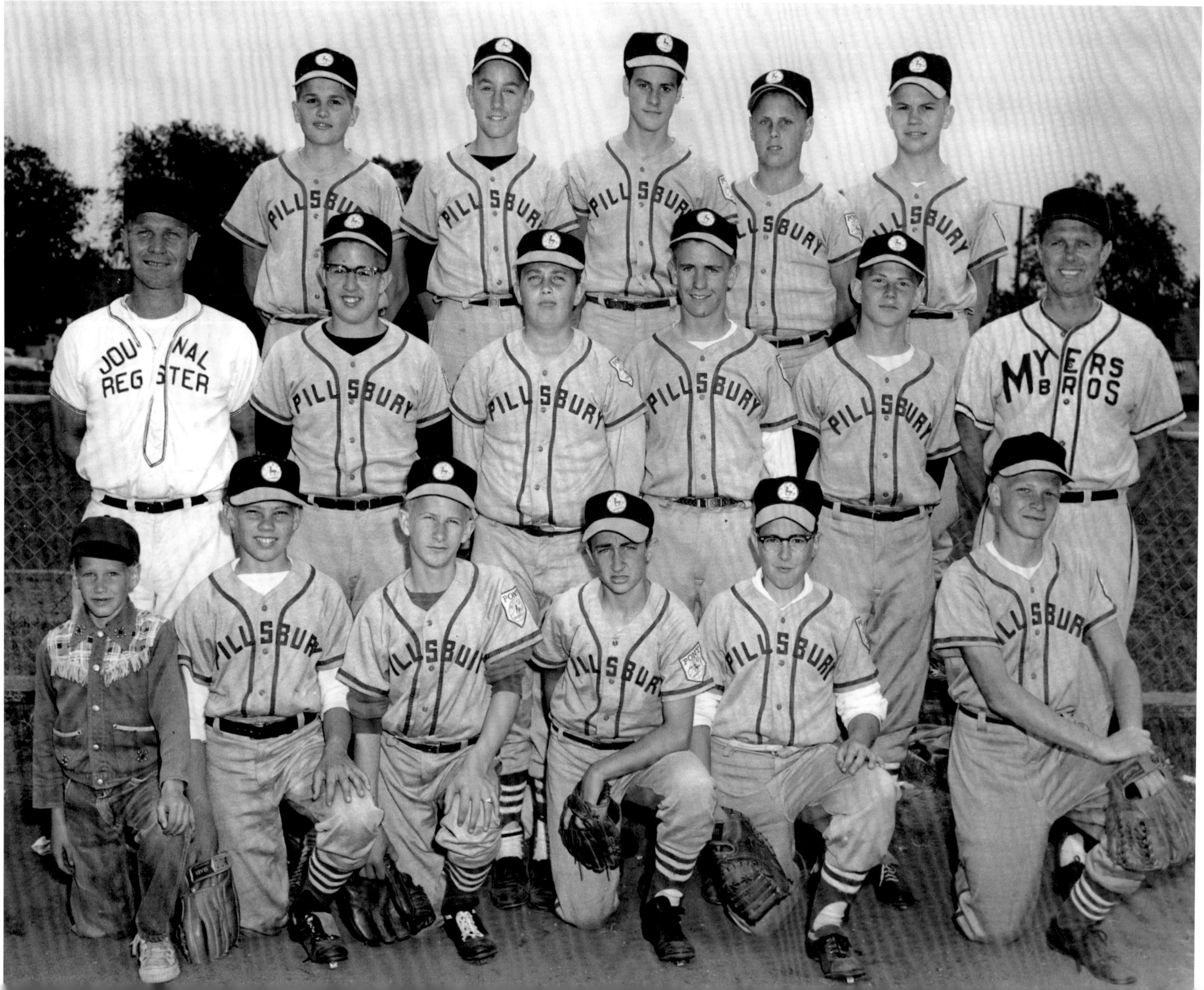
PILLSBURY
MYERS BROS

LEFT: City Water, Light and Power meter readers in front of city hall in 1963. From left: Homer Fox, Andy Saccamano, Bob Laurent, Al Windsor, Louie Capella, Bob Vose, Bob Smith, Tom Skube, Bob Cummins, unidentified and Jim Aubrey. *Courtesy Shirley Laurent*

BOTTOM LEFT: Springfield firefighters during the 1963 March of Dimes fundraiser campaign. Pictured left to right: John Maher (deputy chief), Ken Race (vice president of Local No. 37), Captain Elmer Cartwright (president of Local No. 37) and Art F. Bengel (chief of the Springfield Fire Department). Money received from this event helped to fight infantile paralysis. *Courtesy Fritzi Cartwright*

OPPOSITE: Baseball team photographed at Fairview Park, 1963. Front row, from left: Stan Buecker (bat boy), Randy Carter, John Alexander, Larry Bailey, Bob Egger and Steve Buecker. Middle row: Roger Buecker (coach), Dennis Cartwright, Dick Lamsargis, Mike Constantino, John Groesch, and Elmer Cartwright (manager). Back row: Bill Amerson, John McCoy, Chuck Durning, Mike Fowler, and Jackie Warren. *Courtesy Fritze Cartwright*

BELOW: Don Gunderson, owner, and Harry Gunderson, meat department manager of Gundy's Market, presenting the check for the prize-winning cow at the Illinois State Fair, 1963. *Courtesy Donna Bragg*

ABOVE: The Ramada Inn on Route 66 in 1964. *Courtesy Sangamon Valley Collection, Lincoln Library*

TOP RIGHT: The second street dance for teens, sponsored at the Town & Country Shopping Center in 1964. Nearly 500 teens attended the first event and the attendance nearly doubled for the second street dance event. The Sting Rays provided entertainment for the dance and the president of the merchants association, Jim Diaz, was pleased with the turnout, saying that it was a great outlet for teenage energies. *Courtesy Sangamon Valley Collection, Lincoln Library*

RIGHT: Juniors from Springfield High School at the invitational dance held at the Elks Club Ballroom, 1964. First row, in front: Lynda Swan, Echo Gard, Kathy Henry, Kay Pierce, Cathe Williams, Linda Tucker, Karen Salzman and Vicki Watt. Second row: Bonnie Clark, Darlene Sims, Linda Fryhoff, Sue Isaacs, Cathy Power, Pam Beghyn, Phyllis Porter and Lynn Williams. Third row: George Tepker, Charlie Nemecz, Phil Hinds, Steve Stadtman, Gary Glenn, unidentified, and Mike McClain. Fourth row: Roger Nesch, Oscar Files, Ron Willey, Hal Bast, Craig Allen, Mark Wells, Chuck Tisckos, Terry Springer, and Jerry Cox. *Courtesy Karen Sutton*

ABOVE: A City Water, Light and Power worker is lifted in a snorkel truck to replace a streetlight on South Ninth Street in 1964. *Courtesy Sangamon Valley Collection, Lincoln Library*

LEFT: Panther Creek Bowhunters participants survey their handiwork at a range near Chatham in 1964. *Courtesy Sangamon Valley Collection, Lincoln Library*

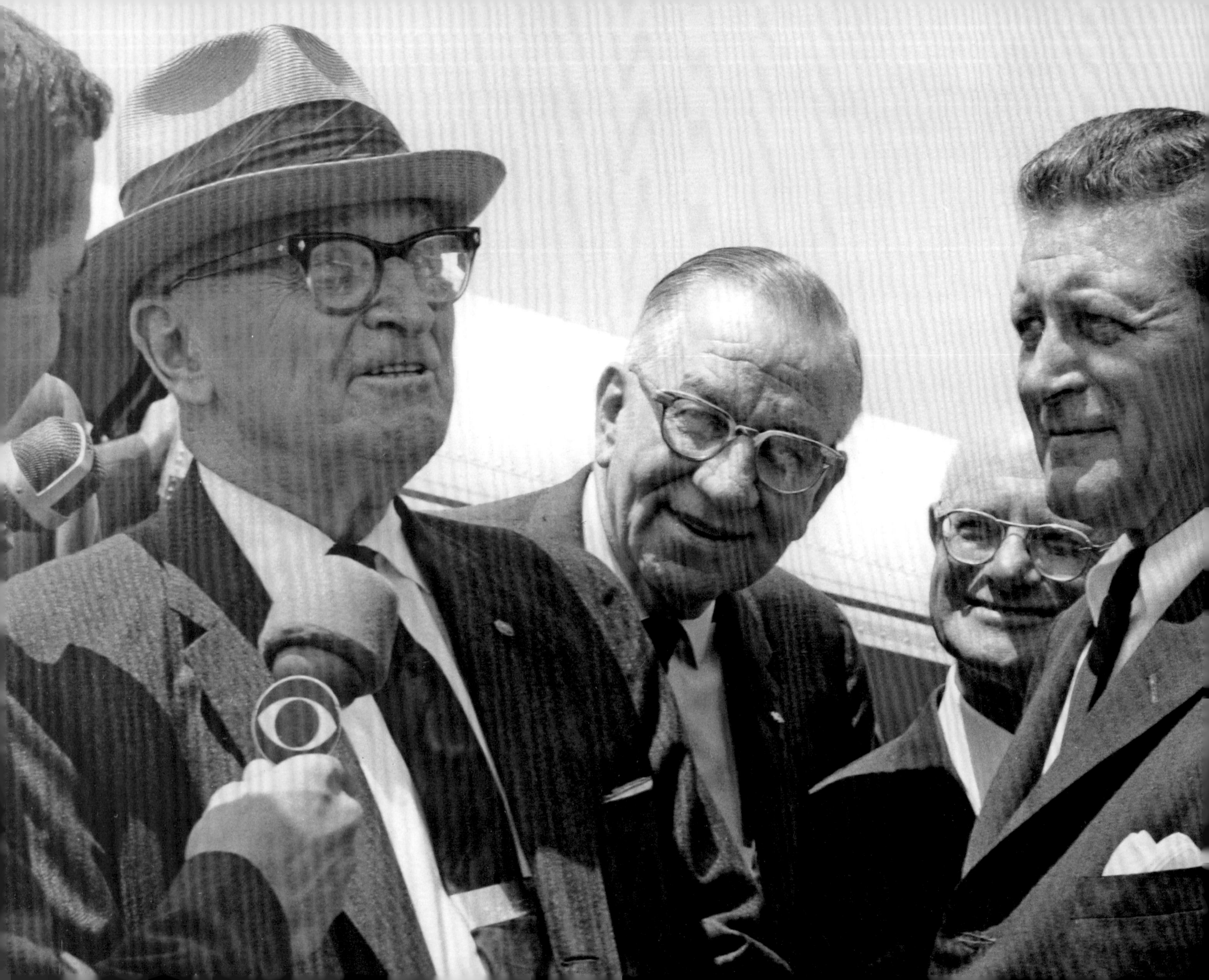

ABOVE: President Lyndon B. Johnson visits Lincoln's Tomb with Gov. Otto Kerner in 1964. *Courtesy Sangamon Valley Collection, Lincoln Library*

TOP LEFT: Charles Chapin, Lillian Reddick, Willa Jean Warless, and Harry Farbman, symphony conductor, at the Chapin home in Chatham, 1964. *Courtesy Nancy Chapin*

LEFT: Mr. and Mrs. Lyndon B. Johnson visiting Springfield in October 1964. *Courtesy Sangamon Valley Collection, Lincoln Library*

FAR LEFT: President Harry Truman says a few words during his visit to Springfield in 1964 as Gov. Otto Kerner, right, and secretary of state candidate Paul Powell listen. *Courtesy Sangamon Valley Collection, Lincoln Library*

ABOVE: Maxwell Township Bridge Project No. 80, Lick Creek, February 6, 1964. *Courtesy Joe Seiz*

RIGHT: Raymond J. Ackerman, assistant engineer of planning for the Illinois Division of Highways, skiing to work at the Statehouse after a snowstorm, January 13, 1964. The Capitol can be seen in the background. The trip from his home on 2128 Fairway Drive took him 45 minutes. *Courtesy Ray Ackerman*

BELOW: A spring hailstorm hits Springfield as a man braves the weather on Sixth Street, facing north, circa 1964. *Courtesy Sangamon Valley Collection, Lincoln Library*

ABOVE: Bob Hinds and Scottie Lewis working for District 6 Division of Highways, using a drill rig for foundation borings, 1964. They did this to create new underground parking and for dismantling and rebuilding the Old State Capitol. *Courtesy Robert L. Hinds*

ABOVE: The Springfield Women's Association of Golf in their group photo at Lincoln Greens, 1964. Starting second in on left, Jennie Rodems; Ida R. Victor; Julie Rowland, city champion; Ann Collins; Judy Meador, city champion; unknown; Bonnie Lensin, city champion; Nancy McCabe; and Connie Felhausen. *Courtesy Ida Ruth Victor*

BELOW: Summer league team picture at the Town & Country Bowling Lanes on MacArthur Boulevard, 1964. Identified are the two women on the right, Marlene Neal and Bertha Wilson. *Courtesy Sandra Colborn*

ABOVE: View of Illinois State Fair festivities, circa 1965. *Courtesy Sangamon Valley Collection, Lincoln Library*

TOP RIGHT: Ostrich race participant encourages his "steed" with his broom to win the race, circa 1965. *Courtesy Sangamon Valley Collection, Lincoln Library*

RIGHT: Children, enjoying their ice cream, take in the large display at the entrance of the Farmland Show at the Illinois State Fair, circa 1965. *Courtesy Sangamon Valley Collection, Lincoln Library*

ABOVE: View of the 200 block of South Sixth Street in the spring of 1965. *Courtesy Sangamon Valley Collection, Lincoln Library*

RIGHT: Flooding at the Tenth Street viaduct on South Grand Avenue in the 1960s. *Courtesy Sangamon Valley Collection, Lincoln Library*

BELOW: Sister M. Gerard of St. John's Hospital presents gifts to Elizabeth, left, and Kathy Coleman, daughters of Mr. and Mrs. Bernard Coleman, after the girls completed a total of 1,451 hours of volunteer service to the hospital. Elizabeth and Kathy were honored along with other candy stripers, who contributed more than 600 hours each to the hospitals, during ceremonies inaugurating Hospital Week in 1965. *Courtesy Sangamon Valley Collection, Lincoln Library*

BELOW: Nearly 150 individual volunteers and organizations assisted in the Mental Health Association's annual "Christmas Wishing Tree" project in 1965. Seen here from left are Beverly Orr, Phyllis Eubanks and Norma Wilkinson. *Courtesy Sangamon Valley Collection, Lincoln Library*

ABOVE: Members of Council 364, Knights of Columbus, chartered two buses in July of 1965 to take a crowd to the St. Louis Cardinals versus the Philadelphia Phillies baseball game at Busch Stadium. From left, front row: Mr. and Mrs. Robert O'Brien, Ann Oliver, Ann Stieren, LaVerne Grant, Bud Simpson, Mr. and Mrs. James Staab, Ted Knust, Don Wendell, Gene O'Brien, Tony Crifast, Bill Yoggerst, Tom Forgas and Dave Yoggerst. Back row: Martin Brady Sr., Martin Brady Jr., Mr. and Mrs. Jack Kornfeld, Mr. and Mrs. Michael Hickey, Val Kerhlikar, Priscilla Tooker, Mr. and Mrs. James Sheehan, Margaret Highfeld, Martha Dalby, Robert Bartlett, Mr. and Mrs. Tracy Neese, Tom Healy, Ivan Shepard, Dorothy Nickelson, Jane Bubnis, Josephine Stritzel, Leo Nichelson, Larry Day and Mr. and Mrs. Larry Markey. *Courtesy Sangamon Valley Collection, Lincoln Library*

RIGHT: Mrs. Leonard Johnson, left, auctions off a package at the Colored Woman's Club auction in the 1960s. The auction was part of a one-day workshop held at the John Hay Homes. Other participants, from left, are Mrs. Gerald Reed, Mrs. Jess Martin, Mrs. Ray Brooks and Mrs. Norma Trede, director of the John Hay Homes. *Courtesy Sangamon Valley Collection, Lincoln Library*

OPPOSITE: The combined choir at Pleasant Grove Baptist Church, circa 1965. In the front row, from left: Lynn Owens, Sandra Gaines, Judy Owens and Ann Grear. Second row: Homer Hubbard, Letha Woolery, Evelyn Durham, Mary Yokem, Sheila Banks, Mrs. Caldonia Carter, Lowery Coleman. Third row: Mrs. Josephine Hearn, Angus Bradley, Mrs. Zora Banks, Mrs. Justine Simmons, John Hubbard. Fourth row: Mrs. Genevieve Wright, Mrs. Mattie Fowler, Mrs. Margaret Criswell, Mrs. Mary Lee Clanton, Miss Edna Ross, Mrs. Selma Renfro, Mrs. Marcella Kirk, John Renfro. Fifth row: Mrs. Alfred Owens, Mrs. Mattie Hale, Mrs. Ollie Hill, Mrs. Florence Lasley, Mrs. Ada Irvine, Mrs. Lillian Walter and Mrs. Vella Hubbard. *Courtesy Sangamon Valley Collection, Lincoln Library*

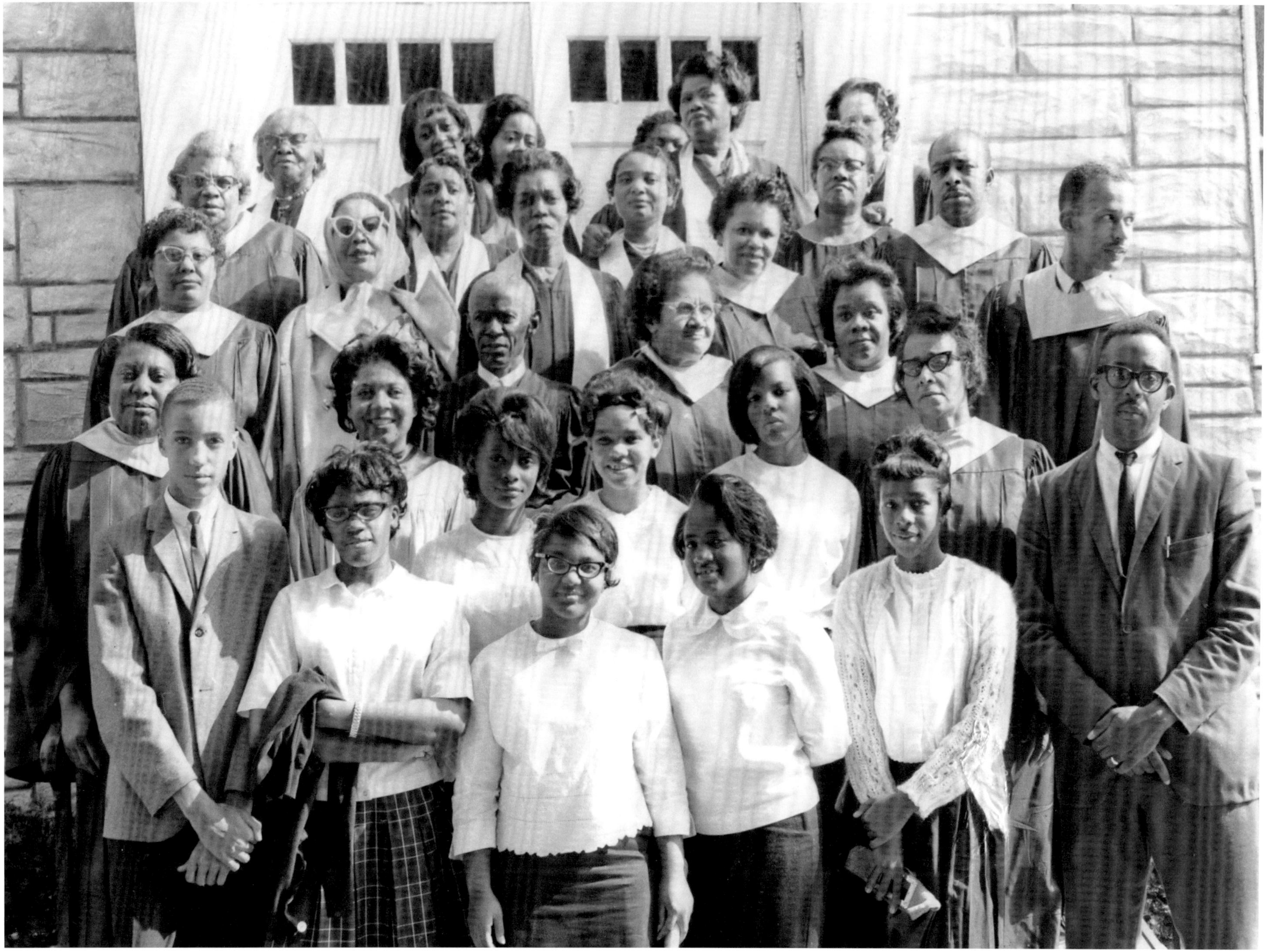

ABOVE: View of the Orpheum Theater at the corner of Fifth and Jefferson streets, 1965. Seen playing at the theater at this time is "The Disorderly Orderly," starring Jerry Lewis. This was taken following the move by the Illinois National Bank to purchase the site for a new motor bank. *Courtesy Sangamon Valley Collection, Lincoln Library*

TOP: Photographer John Fobeck with President Lyndon B. Johnson and the Illinois State Police during his visit in the 1960s. *Courtesy Sangamon Valley Collection, Lincoln Library*

RIGHT: Dr. Martin Luther King Jr. visits Springfield, October 7, 1965. *Courtesy Sangamon Valley Collection, Lincoln Library*

ABOVE: Prairie Farms Little League team at Fairview Park, 19th and Ridgley streets, 1965. Front row, from left: Jim Jarrett, Ken (last name unknown), Kevin Williams, Tony Capranica, and Bob Nika. Second row: John Haines, Mark Pierce, Tim Griffin, Steve Crifasi, Mike Crifasi, Ben Williams, unidentified, and Bobby Gebbardt. Coach Jerry Hamitt is in back. *Courtesy Donna Griffin*

ABOVE: Commodore David M. Wilson and Reva Wilson in the new clubhouse at the Island Bay Yacht Club on Lake Springfield in 1965. *Courtesy Colleen Wilson*

LEFT: Shaheen's Racetrack, circa 1965. *Courtesy Sangamon Valley Collection, Lincoln Library*

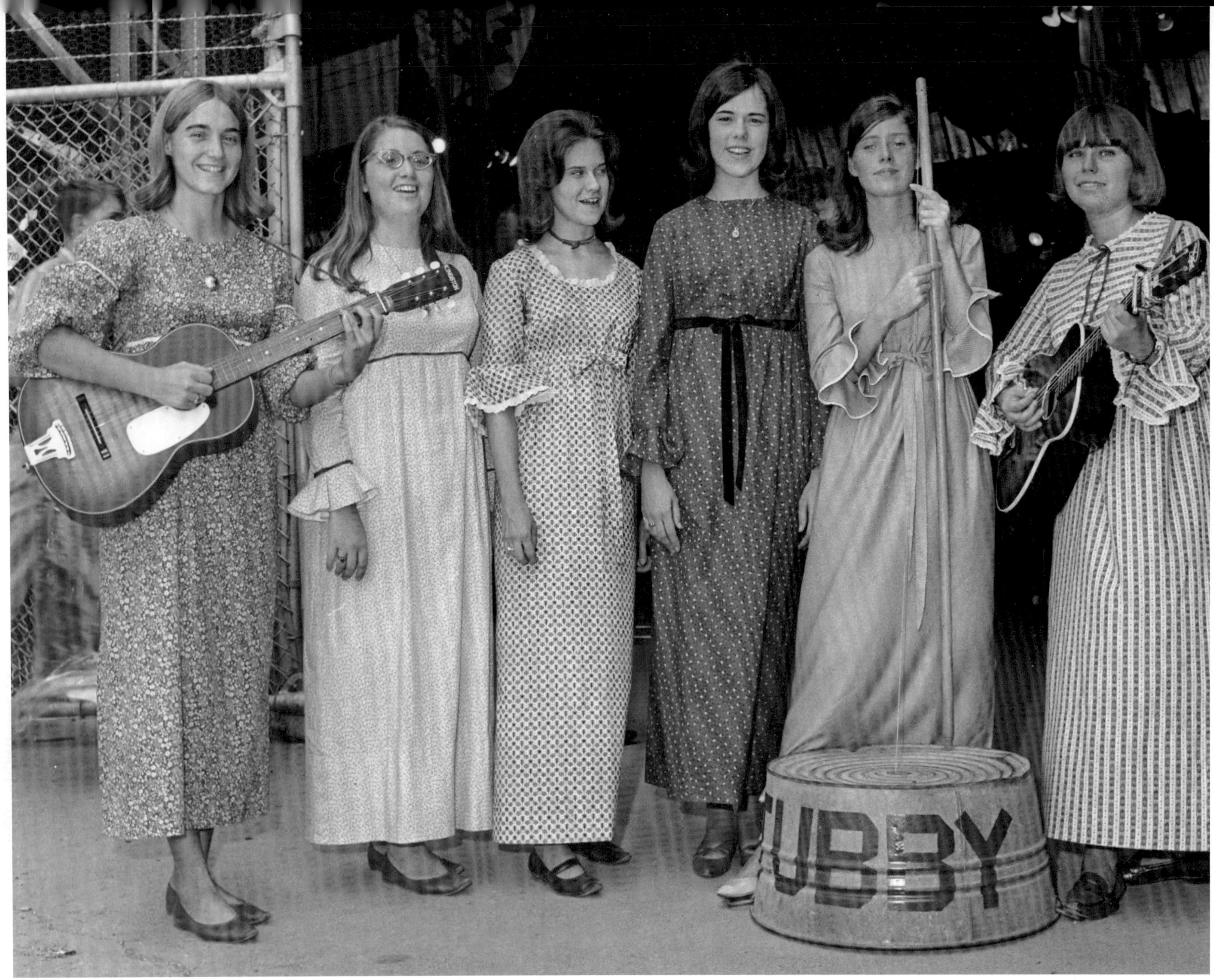
TUBBY

ABOVE: The interior of the Heritage House on South Sixth Street, circa 1965. *Courtesy Maxine Scott*

OPPOSITE: The Folky Niners folk singing group at the Illinois State Fair, 1965. The group was Diane Armstrong, Linda Wallace, Janet Weber, Ann Swango, Kathy Dehen, and Carol Hawker. They performed for various civic groups in the area. *Courtesy Kathy Dehen*

BELOW: Taft's food tent at the fairgrounds, circa 1965. They served milk shakes and hamburgers for 25 cents. *Courtesy Maxine Scott*

ABOVE: The Heritage House on South Sixth Street, circa 1965. *Courtesy Maxine Scott*

BELOW: Ribbon-cutting ceremony for the grand opening of Taft's Drive-In on East Cook Street, circa 1965. Mayor Lester Collins is pictured second from the left. *Courtesy Maxine Scott*

ABOVE: Mr. and Mrs. Glen Farrington, at right, with their daughter and son-in-law, Mr. and Mrs. Richard Heiden, and two grandchildren, Richard Jr. and Michelle on their way to Mass at Blessed Sacrament Catholic Church, circa 1966. *Courtesy Sangamon Valley Collection, Lincoln Library*

RIGHT: Irv Smith shakes hands with Randy "Big Boss" Spencer at the YMCA, 1965. *Courtesy Irv Smith*

FAR RIGHT: The Springfield Municipal Band plays onboard "The Railsplitter" to a group of Springfield residents, May 1966. *Courtesy Sangamon Valley Collection, Lincoln Library*

ABOVE: John Nolan receives his award for St. John's Hospital Employee of the Year in 1966. He is presented his award by Sister M. Jane along with other employees, from left, Joseph Desch, Mrs. Rose Taylor and Robert Wilson. *Courtesy Sangamon Valley Collection, Lincoln Library*

ABOVE: The annual election for the Elks Club in 1966. From left are Gerald C. Stuckey, chairman of the board; William C. Glickert, president; Norman Mack, installing officer; and Sam Dorman, secretary and treasurer. Charles P. Church (not pictured) was elected vice-president. *Courtesy Sangamon Valley Collection, Lincoln Library*

BELOW: Springfield High School Amateur Rocket Club members get ready for launch, June 1966. *Courtesy Sangamon Valley Collection, Lincoln Library*

ABOVE: The Addressograph Department at the State Capitol, 1966. *Courtesy Donna Griffin*

BELOW: Dedication of the Sangamon County Building on May 1, 1966. Gov. Otto Kerner is at the podium. *Courtesy Sangamon Valley Collection, Lincoln Library*

ABOVE: Sisters and laymen gather for the groundbreaking to begin the new addition to St. John's Hospital in November 1967. The section, located at the former east parking lot on Mason Street, was set to house laundry, a power plant and a service building complex and had an estimated cost of $3,768,619. *Courtesy Sangamon Valley Collection, Lincoln Library*

BELOW: Frontiers International installed new officers in 1967. Seated, from left, are Dr. Charles E. Young, president, and Ivan C. Harper, vice-president. Standing are James White, secretary; Harry Hall, treasurer, and Aurthur Ferguson, member of the executive board. *Courtesy Sangamon Valley Collection, Lincoln Library*

ABOVE: Construction of the first phase of St. John's Hospital expansion program in 1968. The multi-million dollar construction and expansion of the hospital facilities took several years. *Courtesy Sangamon Valley Collection, Lincoln Library*

ABOVE: Restoration of the Old State Capitol, October 1967. *Courtesy Sangamon Valley Collection, Lincoln Library*

TOP LEFT: View, facing north, of the reconstruction of the Old State Capitol, September 1967. *Courtesy Carolyn Quinlan*

LEFT: The Bean Soup Club, circa 1967. Seen here are Roy Yung, Walt Roesch, Judge Omer Poos, Judge Paul Verticchio, Judge W. M. Conway, Judge Harry B. Hershey, J.R. Fitzpatrick and Mike Howlett. *Courtesy Sangamon Valley Collection, Lincoln Library*

ABOVE: A 1967 newspaper clipping featuring Captain C.C. Larson, right, in "command" of the "SS Symphony." Larson was promoted to rank of "admiral" during the 10th anniversary ball of the Springfield Symphony Guild. Shown from the left are Dr. Norman Linder, escorting Mrs. Marjorie M. Wagner, founder of the balls, Mrs. Larson and "Admiral" Larson. *Courtesy Joseph Alan Linder*

BELOW: Passengers boarding an Ozark plane on their way to France, Capital Airport, 1967. Identified is Mary Cavanagh turning to wave before boarding. *Courtesy Eleanor Cavanagh*

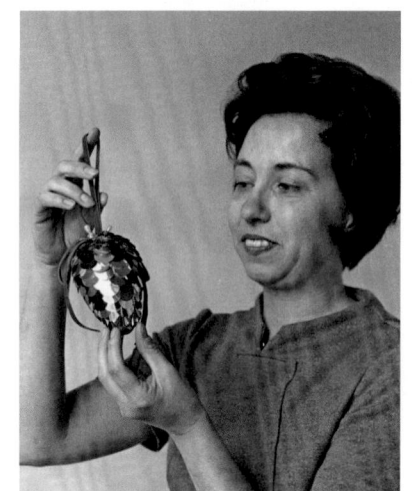

ABOVE: Photo of Mrs. Richard Waughop that was used for a full-page article on the Springfield Ceramics and Crafts Club, 1967. The article was written by Julie Cellini for Pauline Telford's Women's section of The State Journal-Register. *Courtesy Mrs. Richard Waughop*

ABOVE: The Ansar Brass Band, in its heyday, in front of the Ansar Temple, 630 South Sixth Street, 1968. Johnny Watt, potentate, is wearing the dark suit, and Homer Mountz, band director, is in the white suit. *Courtesy Edward and Helen Brooks*

BELOW: Carl Ostermeier campaigning for the office of the Sangamon County recorder in 1968. The photo was taken outside the Rudy Ostermeier Farm, today the Ostermeier Prairie on West Lake Drive. *Courtesy Susan Ostermeier Tesar*

ABOVE: Charles I. Dodd, a well known postman with a reputation for being bighearted, on his route greeting a neighborhood pet, 1968. He befriended many on his southwest side route, even assisting an elderly woman choose a casket, make her funeral arrangements, and then carrying out her wishes when she died. He died on February 6, 2006. *Courtesy Elaine Cormaney*

LEFT: Groundbreaking for the Fraternal Order of Eagles' new building at 910 South Ninth Street, 1968. From left: Wes Fishburn, Bud Fitzpatrick, George Murphy, John Beagles, Joe Shea, Joe Knox, John Vetter, Don Redpath, Harold Bounds, Jerry White, Red McCauley, Eli Dupent, and Waldo McCoy. *Courtesy Joe Shea*

BELOW: The Illinois State Fairgrounds in 1968. *Courtesy Nancy Chapin*

BELOW: Members of the King Family arrived at the Holiday Inn East for their two-day state fair appearance, hot, tired and a little wilted. But the numerous children of the 39-member family seem to have a knack for finding a place to have fun, such as the motel's fountain. Playing it cool, from left are Susannah and Adam King, children of Marilyn King of the King Sisters, and Debra and Stephen Driggs, children of Bill Driggs, one of the eight King Family sons and daughters. The group arrived for the Illinois State Fair in August 1969. *Courtesy Sangamon Valley Collection, Lincoln Library*

ABOVE: Firefighters working to put out the fire at the Schafer Gainer Hatchery at 220 North First Street. The owner, Butch Schafer, tried to go into the building to save his chickens, but the fire department would not allow him, 1969. *Courtesy Sharon Schafer Kording*

ABOVE: Fire at Stern's Furniture Warehouse at 420 East Madison Street on December 26, 1969. *Courtesy Sangamon Valley Collection, Lincoln Library*

LEFT: Twenty-fifth anniversary of the Jerome Jubilee crowning of king and queen at West Grand School, March 15, 1969. Identified standing, from left, are Robert Brownfield; Mark Stroemer; Steve Stroemer; Maenell Thompson; Vernon Shoutz; Mrs. Jon Watson, chair of the Jubilee; and Bill Miller, emcee. Seated are Robyn Hovey, the king, and Barbara Schroeder, the queen. *Courtesy Robyn Hovey*

ABOVE: Marilyn Law and her daughter, Carrie, ice skating in Lincoln Park, 1969. *Courtesy Marilyn Lane*

TOP LEFT: On February 19, 1969, Mayor Nelson Howarth cut the ribbon officially opening the city's new Firehouse No. 8 at Chatham Road and Monroe Street. From left: firefighter Marlyn Geezer, Fire Chief Albert Sommers, president Ronald E. Dudas of the Knox Knolls Improvement Association, Utilities Commissioner John Hunter, Mayor Howarth, Public Health Commissioner Joseph P. Knox, Chief of Police Silver Suarez, Assistant Fire Chief John Bartlett, Civil Defense Director Vernon Strongman and Deputy Fire Chief Charles Johnson. *Courtesy Sangamon Valley Collection, Lincoln Library*

LEFT: The winners of the Elks Ladies Bowling League, the Frye-Williamson Press, Inc. team in May 1969. From left are Mitzi Morris; Virginia Hess; Robert P. Hunley, Frye-Williamson Press representative; Bubble Strawn; Sylvia Coleman; and Marlene Seaborn. *Courtesy Jackie Stites*

Illinois State Journal newsroom or composing, January 1940

News vendor holds Illinois State Journal with headline "Roosevelt Dies," April 12, 1945

Illinois State Journal and Register news carriers, May 1, 1956

Newsroom, September 1957

Illinois State Register newsroom staff, September 26, 1957

Covering our community throughout the years

The State Journal-Register

KEEP YOURSELF CONNECTED.

SJ-R.COM

158

Ace Sign Co.

ESTABLISHED 1940

Since 1940, Ace Sign Co. has created an identity for many Springfield businesses. Franklin G. Horn and his wife, Alvina, started Ace with a pickup truck and modest store front. Hand lettering glass doors, vehicles and oil cloth signs was a way of life, and as technology advanced, so did Ace Sign Co.

Seventy years, four generations of family and many technological advances have changed the way Ace Sign Co. operates, but our passion to take care of our customers and provide them with the highest quality products remains unchanged. From hand lettering to digital printing, from neon to LEDs, and from billboards to full motion video boards, Ace Sign Co.'s philosophy continues to guide the company as a leader in the sign industry.

Today the legacy continues as Ace Sign Co. helps businesses nationwide develop and maintain a professional image with quality-built signage. We thank all those who have supported us over the years and look forward to the many projects ahead.

Ace Sign Co. staff and employees gather for a company photo in front of their new location at 402 N. Fourth St., 1954.

1940
Alvina and Franklin G. Horn founded Ace Sign Co. with their new location at 126 S. Fourth St.

1949
Ace moves to a larger facility and opens a new neon plant at 114 N. Second St.

1953
Ace finds breathing room with the purchase of a new building at 402 N. Fourth St.

1960
Ace purchases their first large installation truck with a manually-operated 45-foot boom.

1983
Ace advances beyond hand painting with the purchase of one of the world's first automated lettering systems.

1971
Ace rises to the occasion with the purchase of a 110-foot hydraulic crane truck.

1990
Ace turns its growing pains into an addition that stretches to the corner of Fourth and Mason.

1993
Ace Sign Co. graphic artists make the transition from hand-drawing to computer-aided design.

1994
Outdoor-grade, full-color digital printing arrive in the graphics department at Ace Sign Co.

1995
Computerized routing equipment adds a new dimension to the expanding capabilities at Ace.

2010
Ace celebrates its 70th year in business!

Joe Bringuet and Glen Gates work off the roof of Illinois National Bank at the corner of Fifth and Washington.

Joe Bringuet operates Ace's first large install truck.

402 N. Fourth St.
Springfield, IL 62702
(217) 522-8417
www.acesignco.com

FRIENDLY CHEVROLET
Established 1965

Friendly Chevrolet has been central Illinois' Chevy dealer since 1965. In 1999, they relocated both stores to the Prairie Crossing Auto Mall on Springfield's west side.

Susan Langheim, owner, is excited about the future of both dealerships especially with all the new products coming from General Motors and Honda.

Friendly Chevrolet has had tremendous success with the new Camaro, Equinox and Traverse and is anxiously anticipating the arrival of the new Chevy Cruze. Recently, General Motors chose Friendly Chevrolet to be the only authorized Saturn service and parts provider in central Illinois. Friendly Chevrolet has added genuine Saturn parts to their inventory and have GM-certified technicians that are here to service your Saturn. Susan Langheim said, "We look forward to welcoming the Saturn customers from Springfield and the surrounding areas to Friendly Chevrolet."

Honda has introduced the new Crosstour for 2010 and the popular Insight hybrid and they continue to have strong sales in the Accord, Civic, CRV and Odyssey lines. Honda of Illinois always receives top customer satisfaction scores for sales and service. Susan Langheim attributes top service scores to having customer-focused managers such as service manager Dick Peters and parts manager Mark Molohon. Both Peters and Molohon have been with Honda of Illinois for 27 years and have always believed in putting the customer first.

Langheim said, "Consumers have told us they want a large selection of vehicles to choose from, and we have listened by stocking several hundred new and pre-owned vehicles every day. Friendly Chevrolet and Honda of Illinois separate themselves from the competition by having a huge selection of vehicles, value pricing, convenient hours and all-day Saturday service. We strive to have a knowledgeable, customer-focused sales staff." She attributes the 59 percent increase in new vehicle sales at Friendly Chevrolet to "Friendly value" pricing. Friendly Chevrolet and Honda of Illinois vow not to be undersold.

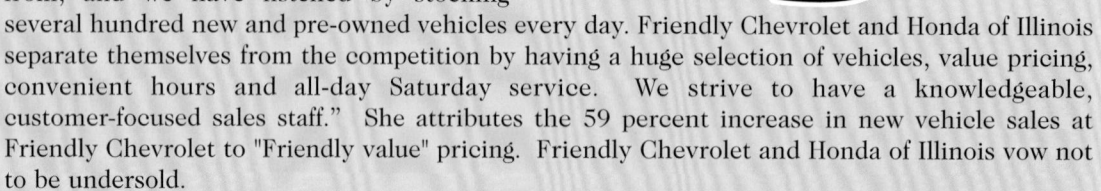

Susan Langheim said it has been an honor to be an automobile dealer in the Springfield area, and she believes in giving back to the community. Friendly Chevrolet and Honda of Illinois have supported various charitable organizations such as the United Way, Hoogland Center for the Arts, Girl Scouts, Big Brothers/Big Sisters to name a few. Friendly Chevrolet is the only central Illinois automobile dealer to host a 30-minute television program showcasing local organizations and promoting their events.

What is Friendly Chevrolet's and Honda of Illinois' business philosophy? Langheim replies, "We want to exceed our customers' expectations every day with each sales, service and parts experience. It is our hope people enjoy visiting our dealerships and will become lifelong customers."

When asked if the best deals really are on Friendly wheels, Langheim answers with an emphatic "Always!"

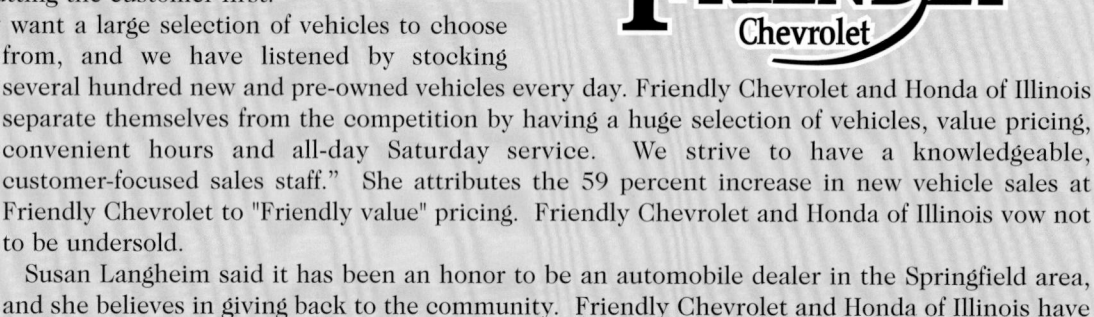

Lincoln Land Development Company

Established 1956

Leonard W. Sapp
"The Imagineer"

From his humble beginnings in the mid 1950s, Leonard W. Sapp – "the Imagineer" – founded Lincoln Land Development Company and began his career of land and commercial real estate development.

First came Val-E-Vue subdivision in 1956 where a pony was given with every lot sold – 59 lots sold in the first 60 days, and all four phases of the subdivision sold out. Then came Lynndale in Sherman, Buckingham Place in Chatham, Plateau Park near Riverton, Golden Acres in Athens, and North Haven in Sherman. In the '60s, other commercial projects were developed – some were apartments, gas stations, restaurants, the Greyhound Bus Station, B.F. Goodrich, and Wedgewood Mobile Home Park, the first Five-Star mobile home park in Illinois. The '60s also saw the start of construction of Fairhills Shopping Center, Springfield's first enclosed mall.

Lincoln Land Development Company's heritage and tradition of first-class development provided new jobs, tax revenues, and improvements in the quality of life for central Illinois residents. All of that continues today with Legacy Pointe, Springfield's first "lifestyle center," bringing new companies and businesses to the community ... "Imagineering" at its best.

Leonard's Humble beginnings. Only owned possession, early '40s.

Typical Sunday pony show at Val-E-Vue, late '50s.

Ribbon cutting of Wedgewood Mobile Home Park, 1964.

Land purchase and beginning earth work, mid '60s.

Lincoln Land Development Company

3601 Wabash, Suite #101 • Springfield, IL 62711
(217) 793-3339 • www.lincolnlanddevco.com

Noonan True Value

Established 1947

Audrey Noonan and Matt Noonan Jr.

NOONAN True Value

Just Ask Rental Commercial Supply Network Grand Rental Station

801 N. Grand Ave. East
(217) 528-1513

510 Bruns Lane
(217) 787-7225

1947
Business started by Matthew A. Noonan Jr. and Audrey E. Noonan at 821 N. Grand Ave. E., Springfield, Ill., as Noonan Hardware.

1950
Joined Cotter & Co., a buying co-op for hardware and related lines. Today known as the True Value Company.

1972
Matthew A. Noonan III joined the business after serving 3½ years in the U.S. Army.

1981
The building at 801 North Grand Ave. E. was purchased to bring the whole retail operation under one roof. This move across the parking lot not only tripled the sales floor space, but also increased the customer parking area to over 100 spaces.

1994
Just Ask Rental was introduced to the retail store.

1997
Expanded into a commercial supply business. Noonan Commercial Supply began with the addition of Matthew A. Noonan IV as the outside salesman.

2000
The purchase of the hardware store at 510 Bruns Lane was completed with the addition of Carl Affrunti as store manager.

2001
Just Ask Rental was installed at the Bruns Lane location.

2008
Grand Rental Station opened at 3031 S. Koke Mill Road.

2010
The family business continues to grow into the future.

821 N. Grand Ave. E., 1961

Matt Noonan II *Matt Noonan III*

Matt Noonan IV *Matt Noonan V*

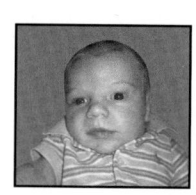

THREE GENERATIONS OF THE MOSCARDELLI FAMILY
SERVING CENTRAL ILLINOIS SINCE 1949

Pleasant Nursery, Inc. defines the meaning of a family-owned business.

In its 61st year, the Moscardelli family has three generations, from grandparents to grandchildren working for the nursery at 4234 W. Wabash Ave.

Started in 1949 by Frank and Agnes Moscardelli, Pleasant Nursery has evolved over the years to include their children: Frank Moscardelli Jr., Sharon Dillon, Dennis Moscardelli, Denise Buscher and Mark Moscardelli; now their grandchildren work at the nursery.

"There is always a family member here," Frank says.

Frank had previously worked in a floral shop before opening Pleasant Nursery, and having the desire to run their own business, Frank and Agnes purchased a small nursery at 1424 N. MacArthur Blvd.

"We started the business from scratch," Frank says. "We worked hard and sacrificed to make it work. It's been a challenge to open a business and keep it going after all these years. We are blessed with good health and a good family."

Today, Pleasant Nursery offers professional design

Frank and Agnes Moscardelli opened their business at 1424 N. MacArthur Blvd. in Springfield

and installation of locally grown nursery stock, maintenance, gifts and florals. Over the years, technology and machines have changed the way they work.

"We started by digging trees by hand," Frank says. "We have evolved to digging the holes by machines and trucks."

Apart from being able to work with family, Frank says being able to work with nature in growing nursery stock is the best part of the business.

When dealing with nature, weather becomes a major obstacle.

"You can't control the weather," Frank says. "And the amount of time spent at the nursery can be challenging. Doing seasonal work can sometimes be a seven-day-a-week job."

The future of Pleasant Nursery is in the hands of the Moscardelli family. Frank and Agnes want nothing more than for the business to be handed down to generations to come.

Frank says he always tried to do the right thing and with the help of God, over the years, it has proven to be the right way to run a business. He is truly thankful for the support of Pleasant Nursery's loyal employees, and both past and present customers.

Pleasant Nursery, Inc.

Illinois State Journal advertising department, January 1940

Pressroom, September 25, 1957

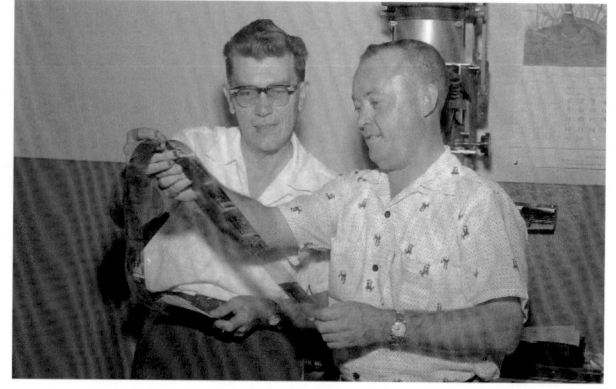

Charlie Bilyeau and Dick Binetsch, September 26, 1957

Platemaking, September 26, 1957

Loading papers onto a delivery truck, September 26, 1957

In 1974, the two long-standing newspapers –
the Illinois State Journal and
the Illinois State Register –
were merged into The State Journal-Register.

Proudly celebrating 179 years
of continuous service as
THE OLDEST NEWSPAPER IN ILLINOIS ™
November 10, 1831-2010

First location on North Walnut Street in Springfield

Then & Now

Chatham Store

Proud to be Central Illinois' Helpful Place since 1951.

George T. and Rosalee Preckwinkle

George W. Preckwinkle and Lucy E. Bagot

In 1951, Robert Bishop purchased the Hill Hardware Store and changed the name to Bishop Hardware. Four years later, in 1955, George T. and Rosalee Preckwinkle purchased a half interest in the store. In 1961, Mr. Bishop retired, selling his remaining interest in the store to the Preckwinkles, and the name of the store was changed to Ace Hardware. The Preckwinkle family has owned and operated the store since 1961.

Keeping in the family tradition, Ace Hardware is now run by the second generation of Preckwinkles, George W. Preckwinkle and Lucy E. Bagot. This brother and sister team have been running the operation since 1980.

Ace Hardware began its long tradition on Walnut Street in 1956. Over the years, the Walnut store has been expanded in size from its original 5,000 sqare feet to its current size of 34,000 sqare feet.

In 1965, the Preckwinkles decided to expand and add a second store in Jacksonville as well as a store in Taylorville in 1972. Company expansion continued with the addition of the store on Wabash Avenue in Springfield in 1973.

In 1989, a fifth store was opened in Normal. Then in 2001, they added Havana's already successful Ace Hardware to the Preckwinkle family. Early 2002 saw the purchase of an eighth store in Carlinville. This store had previously been a family-owned True Value Hardware store. Ace purchased a building in Lincoln and with extensive remodeling, opened a new Ace Hardware in that community in November 2003.

A ninth store was opened in 2005 in Chatham. This store was the first store since 1973 that was built by the company from the ground up. The most recent addition to the Preckwinkle group of stores was a new location in Hillsboro that opened in March 2007.

Through the years, Ace Hardware has won several national awards including Home Center of the Year in 1976, which focused on local family owned and operated stores. With all of the growth and changes, Ace Hardware has remained focused on providing outstanding customer service and quality products. Each of the Preckwinkles' Ace Hardware stores is tailored to meet the needs of its local community. The Preckwinkles are committed to being "the Helpful Place" by providing their customers knowledgeable advice, helpful service and offering quality products they need and promotions the community can relate to. Being family owned and locally operated is a commitment the Preckwinkle family has maintained for the past five decades and looks forward to being an integral part of each community.

The Ace logo has changed throughout the years.

ACE Hardware

- Springfield
- Taylorville
- Normal
- Jacksonville
- Havana
- Carlinville
- Lincoln
- Chatham
- Hillsboro

Index

A

Abraham Lincoln Friendship Train, 41
Abraham Lincoln Sesquicentennial Dinner, 111
Abramitkas, Algimatus, 73
Ace Hardware, 165
Ace Sign Co., 159
Ackerman, Raymond J., 140
Adams, Malcom, 10
Adelman, Bill, 50
Adjusters Association of Central Illinois, 62
Adloff, Grace, 81
Aiello, Mike, 50
Albrecht, Paul, 49
Alexander, John, 135
Allen, Charles, 73
Allen, Craig, 136
American Legion social club, 66
Amerson, Bill, 135
Amrhein, Carl, 82
Anderson, Clavin, 126
Anderson, Mr. and Mrs., 71
Anderson, Otha, 95
Anheuser-Busch Co. employees, 61
Ansar Brass Band, 154
Arisman, Charles, 81
Armbruster, Bernard, 128
Armstead, Tom, 86
Armstead-Fisher, Donna, 80
Armstrong, Diane, 148
Armstrong, Mike, 81
Armstrong, Mrs. Clarence, 110
Arnold, Donna, 113
Arvin, LeRoy, 116
Aschaur, Ann, 128
Ashton, Jim, 128
Atchinson, Rosa, 126
Aubrey, Jim, 135
Aufmuth, Rosemary, 107

B

Babcock, Helen, 112
Babiak, Robert, 21
Babiak, Walter, 21
Bacall, Lauren, 68
Bagot, Lucy E., 165
Bailey, Larry, 135
Baldoni, John, 80
Baldwin, Kendall, 91
Bancroft, Eva Mae, 122
Banks, Monroe, 54
Banks, Ozzie, 34
Banks, Sheila, 145
Banks, Zora, 145
Barger family, 73
Barlow, Jack, 40
Barlow, Mary Rose, 40
Baron, Mrs. Van, 131
Barrett, Edward, 46
Barrow, Bruce, 40
Barrow, Carolyn, 40
Barrow, Ronald, 40

Bartlett, John, 157
Bartlett, N., 51
Bartlett, Robert, 144
Barton, Donald, 95
Barton, Juanita, 95
Barton, Terry, 82
baseball teams, 34, 72, 123, 124, 134, 147
basketball team, 50
Bast, Hal, 136
Baughn, Karen, 91
Bax, John, 81
Beagles, John, 155
Bean Soup Club, 153
Beard, Evelyn, 40
Beatty, David, 21
Beaumont, Jesse, 73
Beck, Jack, 126
Becker, Carylyn, 85
Becker, Conrad F., 82
Becker, Paul, 112
Beggs, Daniel, 73
Beghyn, Pam, 136
Bell, Louise, 21
Bengel, Art F., 135
Bennett, Frank, 21
Bettis, Beverly, 126
Bianco, Dominic, 84
Bianco, Jon, 84
Bianco, Rose Sinitra Termine, 84
Bick, Harry, 103
Bish, Edgar, 95
Bivin, Bonigail, 52–53
Black, Sandy, 113
Blackston-Moore, Jean, 80
Blair, Aaron, 73
Blake, Donald, 27
Blake, Harvey, 40
Blake, Joann Sargeant, 40
Blalock, Ralph "Big Toe," 128
Blalock, Richard, 21
Blauvelt, Sara, 81
Bluhm, John, 112
Blush, Paul, 64
Boardman, Chris, 91
Bogardus, R., 86
Bogart, Claire, 104, 107
Bogart, Humphrey, 68
Boggs, Lucille, 21
Bolinger, James P. "Bunk House," 128
Bolton, Chuck, 113
Bommarito, Joe, 120
Bond, Rose, 83
Bonefeste, Joe, 120
Bordan, May, 51
Bose, Mary, 21
Bosie, Bill, 81
Boswell, Rudy, 34
Bounds, Harold, 155
bowling teams, 9, 141, 157
Boyce, Carol Sue Wilcoxson, 72
Boyd, Albert, 95
Boyle, Charles A., 82
Boy Scouts, 96, 128, 131
Bradley, Angus, 145
Bradley, Bip, 126
Bradley, Christine, 83
Bradley, Martha, 112
Bradley, Mongolia, 95
Brady, Martin, 144

Braham, Barbara, 73
Brahler, Irene, 80
Brahler, Jim, 81
Brammer, Patricia, 73
Brancato, C., 86
Brancato, P., 51
Brandon, Charles, 73
Brandt, Willy, 111
Brawner, Ina, 21
Brents, Betty, 69
Brents, Enos, 34
Bridges, Jan, 112
Bridgewater, Donna, 105
Bridgewater, Paula Kay, 128
Bringuet, Joe, 159
Bristow, Sara, 50
Broaddus, Dick, 126
Brockmeier, Rev. John, 50, 80
Broida, Rick, 81
Brooks, Mrs. Ray, 144
Brown, Delores, 73
Brown, Douglas M. "Deacon," 128
Brown, Floyd, 110
Brown, Kenneth, 34
Brown, Othel, 69
Brown, Pat, 81, 126
Brown, Paul, 21
Brown, Sue, 122
Brown, Wayne, 21
Brownfield, Robert, 156
Brownies, 91
Brust, Bob, 64
Bryant, Judy, 122
Bubnis, Jane, 113
Buchanon, Craven, 95
Buecker, Roger, 135
Buecker, Stan, 135
Buecker, Steve, 135
Bullard, Anita, 122
Bullard, Linda, 122
Burk, Paul, 25
Burke, Kathy, 104
Burns, Virginia, 21
Burris, David, 40
Burris, John, 73
Burt, Beverly, 73
Burtle, Susan, 128
Burton, Betsy Fitzpatrick, 82
Burton, Sandy, 128
Busch, Maurice, 126, 128
Bush, Susan, 101
Butcher-Brahler, Irene, 80
Byers, Ray, 31

C

Cadigan, Dan, 81
Calandrino-Rogers, Clara, 80
Calkins, Harold and family, 49
Call, Juanita, 83
Caloway, Ron, 81
Calvin, William D., 68
Campbell, Hugh and Doris, 116
Campbell, Leslie, 91
Campbell, Linda, 91, 101
Campbell, Mrs., 58, 91
Canselar family, 13
Capella, Louie, 135
Capin, Chick, 27
Capranica, Tony, 147
Caprinica, Louise "Beja," 34

Cardoni, L., 86
Carmean, Jim, 113
Carpentier, Charles, 33, 82, 92, 99
Carpentier, Susan Jane, 99
Carr-Rechner, Donna, 80
Carter, Caldonia, 145
Carter, Randy, 135
Cartwright, Dennis, 135
Cartwright, Elmer, 135
Carver, J., 86
Carver family, 22
Castle, Latham, 82
Cathedral Boys High School Variety Show, 73
Catlin, Donna Arnold, 113
Cavanagh, Mary, 154
Cecilia, Sister Mary, 80
Cessna, Charles E., Jr., 31
Chambers, Theodore, 73
Chambers, W. Arnold, 116
Chance, Harold D. "Ropin'", 128
Chaney, Cedell, 34
Chapin, Charles, 139
Chapman, John W., 105
Chase, Ted, 120
Chiles, Clarence B., 33
Chiola-Davis, Donna, 80
Chorn, Ed, 128
City Water, Light and Power employees, 126, 135, 137
Civil Defense Communications Center employees, 63
Civil Service Establishment Board, 110
Clanton, Mary Lee, 145
Clark, Billy, 98
Clark, Bonnie, 136
Clark, Scott, 21
Clark, T., 72
Clark D. Franke Jr. employees, 112
Clowers, Margaret, 81
clown show on WICS-TV, 89
Cloyd, Ron, 21
Coady, Wayne, Jr., 112
Cobb, Janet, 64
Coe, Joann, 40
Coe, Sam, 82
Coleman, Albert, 110
Coleman, Elizabeth, 143
Coleman, Kathy, 143
Coleman, Lowery, 145
Coleman, Mr., 34
Coleman, Sylvia, 157
Collins, Ann, 141
Collins, Larry, 40
Collins, Lester, 149
Collins, Mandy, 112
Colored Women's Club, 144
communion classes, 34, 39, 83
Coniglio, Joseph, 80
Conley, Emma Lee Stewart, 69
Conley, Kermit, 91
Constantino, Mike, 135
Contrall, Deborah, 101
Conway, W. M., 153
Conwill, Joyce, 126
Cook, Dave, 66
Cook, Marjorie, 39, 73
Cook, Marylin, 73
Cook, Patricia, 39
Cooke, Don, 108

Coombs, Janie, 105
Coontz, Donald, 73
Cooper, Robert, 112
Copeland, Fred, 95
Cormaney, Lewis, 112
Cornelius, Allan, 126
Cornman, Bill, 81
Cottage Hill School students, 65
Cousin, Vincent, 40
Covents, Rene, 57
Cox, Jerry, 136
Craig, George H., 52–53
Craig, Julia, 89
Cravens, Clarence, 98
Crawford, Calvin O., 110
Crifasi, Mike, 147
Crifasi, Steve, 147
Crifast, Tony, 144
Crim, Williams, 110
Criswell, Margaret, 145
Croft, H.O., 112
Croft, James, 21
Croll, Joann, 40
Crookshank, Hal, 112
Cross, Hugh W., 33
Culbertson, Eleanor, 83
Cullen, Mrs. Geo. 58
Culp, Mary, 81
Cummins, Bob, 135
Cummins, Nancy, 80
Curby, Susan, 122

D

Dabney, Lyle, 95
Dalbey, David, 29, 78
Dalbey, Jim, 29
Dalby, Martha, 144
Daley, Pat, 50
dance classes and groups, 18, 19, 51, 69, 101
Darlin, Johnny, 125
Davenport, Robert, 21
Davis, Donald, 21
Davis, Donna, 80
Davison, Cynthia, 81, 98
Day, Larry, 144
DeBeaulieu, Maryann, 50
Dehen, Kathy, 148
De Jaegher, Gerald, 57
De Keere, August, 57
Delaney, P., 51
Dempsey, Jack, 69
Denham, Maryann, 73
Denton, Bob, 86
DeRosa, Bill, 64
DeRosa, John, 64
DeRosa, Mike, 64
Desch, Joseph, 150
DeYoung, Eleanor, 39
Dietel, John, 64
Divine, Lila, 110
Dixon, Mr. and Mrs. Chester, 66
Dobbs, Hugh J., 33
Doby, Allene, 73
Dodd, Charles I., 155
Dodsworth, Gene, 122, 126
Donaldson, Sharon, 107
Donner, Mrs. Clay M., 110
Dorland, Robert, 73
Dorman, Sam, 151

Douglas, Betty Brents, 69
Douglas, Paul, 82
Dudas, Ronald E., 157
Dudley, Charles, 69
Duffy, Helen Quinnigan, 34
Duncan, Leroy, 120
Dunham, James, 126
Dunlevy, Bryan, 81
Dupent, Eli, 155
Durham, Evelyn, 145
Durning, Chuck, 135

E

Earl, Jack, 73
Earl, Joel, 73
Earl, William, 73
Earles, Gary, 126, 128
Earles, Linda, 122, 128
Eckhoff, Frances, 80
Ecklund, Linda, 91, 101
Eddington, Darlene, 105
Edgecomb, Jay, 104
Edson, William, 73
Edwards, Dan, 21
Edwards, Robert R., 33
Edwards, Valerie, 126, 128
Egger, Bob, 135
Eielson, Harry, 33
Eisenhower, Dwight, 52–53, 76
Eisenhower, Mamie, 76
Eldridge, Janet, 126
Elks Club, 151
Elledge, G. Wade, 73
Ellis, Shirley, 21
Embree, Cindy, 104
Estill, Hazel, 83
Etter, Dora, 83
Eubanks, Phyllis, 143
Evans, B., 72
Evans, Billy, 82
Evans, Clarence R. "Highpockets," 128
Evans, Kathleen "Babe" Paoni, 34
Evans, Leo, 80
Evans, Ruby, 112
Ewing, David, 81

F

Faeth, Juanita, 83
Faeth, Vickie, 122
Fairway Golf Club Tournament members, 95
Farber, Mary, 91
Farbman, Harry, 139
Farrington, Mr. and Mrs. Glen, 150
Faulkner, W., 86
Fehrholz, R., 83
Feitshans High School students, 86
Felhausen, Connie, 141
Ferguson, Arthur, 152
Feuer, Sara, 112
Fiersten, Rick, 126
Files, Oscar, 136
Filsak-Williams, Barbara, 80
Findley Girls, 120
Finn, James, 80
fires, 22, 30, 62, 94, 102, 156
First United Methodist Church choir, 97
Fischer, Carl, 81
Fishburn, Frank, 40

Fishburn, Wes, 155
Fisher, Donna, 80
Fisher, J., 72
Fitzpatrick, Betsy, 82
Fitzpatrick, Bud, 155
Fitzpatrick, James R., 82, 153
Fitzpatrick, Mrs. James, 82
Fiush, D., 72
Fix, Richard, 50
Flaretty, Bob, 64
Fleer, Eva, 83
Fleming, Kelly, 81
floods, 24, 109, 143
Flour Mill Workers Union leaders, 33
Flynn, Danny, 128
Fobeck, John, 146
Folkerts, Linda, 101
Folky Niners singers, 148
Fontegne, Harry, 57
football teams, 86
Ford, Toni, 81
Forgas, Tom, 144
Foster, Carol, 73
Foster, Dorothy Logan, 69
Foster, Martha, 126, 128
Foster, Nancy, 126, 128
Foster, Susanne, 40
Foster, T., 86
Fowler, Mattie, 145
Fowler, Mike, 135
Fox, Homer, 135
Frankie Leonard Orchestra members, 120
Franklin, Janet, 21
Frankowiak, Shirley, 104
Frantz, Bob, 64
Frenz, Jack, 120
Fribley, John W., 33
Frick, Tom, 81
Friendly Chevrolet, 160
Fries, Pam, 104
Frontiers International officers, 152
Fryhoff, Howard, 116
Fryhoff, Linda, 136
Fulgenzi, Karen, 93
Fulgenzi, Margaret, 93
Fulgenzi family, 44
Furrow, Betty, 21

G

Gager, Patricia, 73
Gaines, Sandra, 145
Galassi, Toni, 34
Galassi, Trillie, 34
Gallant, Neva, 83
Gangitano, Theresa, 80
Gard, Echo, 136
Gardner, J., 86
Garden Club members, 110
Garecht, Bill, 50
Garvey, Irene, 110
Gates, Glen, 159
Gebbardt, Bobby, 147
Gedney, Mr. and Mrs. Eldon, 14
Geezer, Marlyn, 15
Gent-Petrella, Charleene, 80
Gentry, Dorothy, 34
Gerard, Sister M., 143
Gerula, Mike, 99
Giachetto, Domenic "Mesquite," 128

Giao, Raymond, 40
Gibbins, J., 86
Gibson, F., 86
Giffen, D. Logan, 33
Gilbert, William, 34
Gillock, Liz, 34
Gilmore, Glen, 23
Giovagnoli, Hugo, 100
Girl Scout Camp Widjiwagan, 64, 67
Girl Scouts, 118
Glenn, Gary, 136
Glenn, Rev. Donald, 81
Glenwood High School students, 126, 128
Glickert, Loretta, 73
Glickert, William C., 151
Gorens, Bobby, 34
Gorens, Jack, 24
Gorens' School of Beauty Culture, 20
Gourley, Mrs. J.T., 58
Gramlich, Gary, 81
Gramlich, Margaret, 50
Grandview Club Reunion, 59
Granoski, Ellen, 101
Grant, LaVerne, 144
Grant, Sandy Black, 113
Gray, J., 86
Gray, Mrs. Miles, 110
Gray, Tom, 104
Grear, Ann, 145
Greeley, Bill "Grizzly," 128
Green, Dwight, 33, 41
Green, J., 86
Greenfield, David, 40
Griffin, Ken, 86
Griffin, Kenneth and Donna, 107
Griffin, Tim, 147
Griffith, William, 21
Griffiths, Lynn, 122
Grobelnik, Fred, 80
Groesch, Don, 123, 129, 135
Gunderson, Don, 123, 129, 135
Gunderson, Donna Lea, 129
Gunderson, Harry, 135
Gunderson, Kathy Sue, 129
Gunderson, Mary Jane, 129

H

Haak, Richard, 128
Haaker, Carol, 120
Hack, Alice, 95
Hack, Henry, 95
Hager, Ralph, 113
Haines, John, 147
Hale, Mattie, 95
Hall, Harry, 152
Hallowell, James, 80
Hamitt, Jerry, 147
Hammons, Paul, 34
Hamner, George, 95
Hamner, Mrs. Charley, 95
Hanner, Mildred, 21
Hardy, Enos, 95
Hardy, Gladys, 95
Harlan, Verna, 40
Harlow, Gerald, 73
Harper, Helen, 95
Harper, Ivan, 95, 152
Harris, C., 86
Harris, Fred L., 95

Harris, Gladys, 95
Harrison, John, 122
Harris subdivision homeowners, 69
Harshaw, Wayne, 113
Harvard Park Dad's Club Minstrel Show, 69
Harvard Park Elementary School students, 21
Harvell, Patricia, 105
Hashman, Yvonne, 19
Hawker, Carol, 148
Hawkins, Harold "Cy," 128
Hayes, Tom, 81
Hays, Don, 50
Hazel Dell School students, 81
Head, Pat, 126
Healy, Tom, 144
Hearn, Josephine, 145
Heger, Patricia, 21
Heiden family, 150
Heisler, Bob, 81
Helms, Charles, 73
Henderson, Harold, 100
Hendricks, Archie, 9
Hendricks, John, 82
Henry, Kathy, 136
Henry, Raymond, 34
Henry, William C., 31
Herchy, Lawrence, 73
Herchy, Ronald, 73
Hershey, Harry B., 153
Herter, Peggy, 101
Heselton, Elizabeth, 105
Hess, Richard, 107
Hess, Virginia, 157
Hewitt, Coleman, 48
Hewitt, Mark, 48
Hewitt, Suzanne, 91
Hickey, Mr. and Mrs. Michael, 144
Highfeld, Margaret, 144
Hiler, Judy, 80
Hill, Mrs. Ollie, 145
Hill, Peggy, 73
Hinckle, Dick, 81
Hinds, Bob, 141
Hinds, Pauline, 83
Hinds, Phil, 136
Hinsey, Raleigh, 64
Hirstein, Todd, 104
Hobbs, John, 34
Hodge, Margaret, 91
Hoelzel, Donald, 21
Hoffman, Eurel, 120
Hohimer, Ron, 128
Hollis, R., 86
Holtzworth, Jim, 40
Homier, J., 72
Homiller, Norman C., 112
Honda of Illinois, 160
Hoogland, C.C., 116
Hoover, Jim, 78
Horn, Jack, 34
Horney, Ruth, 104
Hovey, Robyn, 156
Howard, Marian, 83
Howard, Mary, 73
Howarth, Nelson, 77, 87, 96, 157
Howlett, Mike, 153
Hubbard, Gerry, 21
Hubbard, Homer, 145

Hubbard, John, 145
Hubbard, Leonard, 34
Hubbard, Vella, 145
Huffman, Trillie Galassi, 34
Hughes, James, 73
Hughes, Joe, 34
Hughes, Shirley, 74, 98
Hughett, Irene, 69
Hummer Mfg. employees, 66
Hunley, Robert P., 157
Hunt, Cloyd, 126
Hunter, Carolyn, 40
Hunter, Charles, 73
Hunter, Dale, 10, 78
Hunter, John, 157
Hurwitz, Lynn, 104
Hutchinson, S. Phil, 82
Hutton, U.R., 51
Hyatt, James, 27
Hyatt, Wanda, 73
Hyde, Jean, 101
Hyde, Sara Jean, 91

I

Ice, Ina Rae, 83
Illinois Capitennial celebration, 100, 101, 104, 105
Illinois state employees, 73, 90, 151
Illinois State Fair, 24, 26, 30, 31, 35, 44, 45, 48, 49, 56, 74, 78, 82, 92, 106, 122, 142, 148, 149, 155
Illinois State Journal-Register, 164
Inslee, Lloyd, 70
International Shoe Co. employees, 60
Irvine, Ada, 145
Irwin, Janet, 105
Isaacs, Sue, 136
Isom, Charles, 34

J

Jackson, Anna Mae, 95
Jackson, Gloria, 36
Jackson, Naomi, 73
Jackson, V., 51
Jacob, Art, 70
James, B., 72
Jane, Sister M., 150
Jannessee-Seiders, Rita, 80
Jansen, Bea, 73
Jarrett, Jim, 147
Jarvis, Joann, 40
Jenkins, Mr. and Mrs., 66
Jenot, Carolyn, 93
Jepson, Harold, 52–53
Jepson, Margaret, 52–53
Jerome Jubilee, 156
Johnson, Charles, 157
Johnson, Dale, 113
Johnson, James, 8
Johnson, Lady Bird, 139
Johnson, Lyndon B., 139, 146
Johnson, M.J., 51
Johnson, Mrs. Leonard, 144
Johnson, Ward M. "Sangamo Sage," 128
Jones, Alex, 126
Jones, J. David, 33
Jones, Jim, 81
Jordan, Norma, 80

K

Kane, Harold, 21
Kane, R., 72
Kane, Ron, 84
Kapp, Buddy, 42, 82
Kapp, John W., Jr., 33
Kaylor, Sonya, 69
Kays, A.R., 31
Kelly, J., 86
Kelly, Jay, 38
Kelly, Rev. Luke, 50
Kemp, Carol, 39
Kemp, Tom, 39
Kennedy, John F., 132, 133
Kerhlikar, Val, 144
Kerner, Otto, 138–39, 151
Kerr, Chuck, 128
Kerschieter, Rene, 57
Kienzler, Richard, 110
Kimball, Douglas, 112
Kincaid, Mary Lee, 21
King, Martin Luther, Jr., 146
King family, 155
Kinney, Mrs., 40
Kirk, Marcella, 145
Kiska, Melba, 98
Knights of Columbus, 144
Knock, Dan, 81
Knox, Joe, 155, 157
Knox, Katie, 67
Knust, Ted, 144
Kolbialka, H., 72
Konrad, Lillian, 83
Kornfeld, Mr. and Mrs. Jack, 144
Krebs, Joseph, 80
Krell, Alvin, Jr., 21
Krell, Charles, 128
Krell, Janice, 122, 126, 128
Krouse, Joe, 64
Krska, Patsy, 40
Krueger, Bob, 126
Kuntzman, Dorothy, 112

L

Lake Club employees, 100
Lake Springfield Christian Assembly High School students, 43
Lambert, C. Duane, 26
LaMotte, J., 86
Lamsargis, Dick, 135
Lancaster, Mrs. Sam, 110
Lane, Judy, 85
Lane, Marilyn, 85
Lane, Marilyn Lou, 40
Langenfeld, Clifford, 21
Langenfelt, Mr., 72
La Roi Frozen Foods Co. employees, 61
Larson, Guy, 80
Larson, Mr. and Mrs. C.C., 154
Larson, Nan, 83
Lascody, Robert, 80
Lasey, Mrs. Don, 58
Lashbrook, Nancy Richter, 120
Lasley, Florence, 145
Laurent, Bob, 98, 135
Lauterback, John, 21
Law, Carrie, 157
Law, Marilyn, 157
Lawler, Paul, 113

Lawrence School students, 104
Layendecker, Kenneth, 80
Leach, Lum, Jr., 21
Leahy, Margaret "Missy," 128
Leathers, Daniel "Tony," 113
Leathers, Laverne Wilson, 113
Lee, Ann, 128
Lee, JoAnn, 98
Lee, Tex, 129
Leistner, Louise, 83
Leka, James, 82
Lensin, Bonnie, 141
Lepper, Joe, 50
Lepper-Zink, Ellen, 80
Lewis, B., 86
Lewis, James, 80
Lewis, Patti, 128
Lewis, Patty, 126
Lewis, Scottie, 141
Liles, Paulette, 126
Lincoln Elementary School students, 73
Lincoln Land Development Co., 161
Lincoln Ordnance Depot employees, 23
Linden, Owen, 124
Linder, Norman, 154
Lindsay, Bernie, 50
Lindsley, Janet, 101
Liner, Norman, 80
Liner-Jordan, Norma, 80
Lingle, Mrs. Myron K., 110
Livingston, J. E., 95
Lockard's Jewelry Store employees, 70
Lockhart, Charles, 95
Loew, Diane, 104
Loew, Frances, 104
Loew, Gloria, 104
Loew, Peggy, 104
Logan, Dorothy, 69
Logan, Jan, 122
Lohman, Martin B., 33
Long, Mary Jean, 128
Longen, Robert, 80
Lou, Peter, 11
Loveless, Kay Wicks, 105
Lucas, Scott, 46
Luedtke, Walter, 98
Luers, Mrs. Fred, 58
Lutes, R., 86
Lutz, Henry M., 33, 128
Lynes, Marion R., 112

M

Mack, Norman, 151
Macleod, Irene, 80
Maher, John, 135
Mahoney, Ed, 112
Mahoney, Joe, 113
Mallory, Priscilla, 69
Malone-Martin, Mabel, 80
Manci, Louis, 73
Marconi, F., 86
Marie, Caroline, 104
Markey, Mr. and Mrs. Larry, 144
Marr, Gary, 128
Martin, Bob, 50
Martin, Frank, 88

Martin, Mabel, 80
Martin, Mrs. Jess, 144
Masters, Mary Jane, 77
May, Jim, 122
McAfee, Roy, 128
McAvoy, Barbara, 122
McBrian, Nancy, 122
McBride, Wanda, 73
McCabe, Nancy, 141
McCall, A.B., 48
McCauley, Red, 155
McClain, Marianne, 91
McClain, Mike, 136
McClain, William, 73
McClelland, Logan, 126
McCloud, Donna, 73
McCord, Martha, 104
McCoy, John, 135
McCoy, Waldo, 155
McCurley, Janet, 91
McDonald, Judi, 122
McElroy, William, 110
McFadden, Kathleen, 93
McGlothlin, Mary, 73
McGrath, Leo, 50
McHenry, N., 86
McIntyre, James R., Sr., 58
McKnight, Helena, 126
McLean, Marilyn, 126
McNally, Carol, 50
Meador, Judy, 141
Meaney, Larry, 82
Medley, David, 40
Meiron, Betty, 45
Meiron, Helen, 45
Meiron, Sofie, 45
Meisenbacher, B., 86
Meissner, Johanna, 83
Mendenhall, Gary, 126
Mendenhall, Wayne, 128
Mennis, Mr., 40
Merci, Charles, 57
Meredith, Nadine, 73
Merriweather, Harriett, 95
Meyer, Mary Ann, 48
Midden, Charles, 92
Milam, Larry, 82
Milburn, B., 86
Miller, Bill, 156
Miller, Glen and Mabel, 56
Miller, John "Jack," 80
Miller, Richard, 73
Miller, William, 21
Milner, Mary, 126
Misplay-Watkins, Jacqueline, 80
Mitchell, Frank, 131
Mitts, Roy, 126
Monohan, B., 51
Monroney, Radene, 120
Montgomery, Bernice, 73
Montgomery, Juanita, 105
Moore, Emma, 36
Moore, Irma Kay, 128
Moore, James, 80
Moore, Jean, 80
Moore, William, 21
Moriconi, Frank, 101
Morris, Donna, 93
Morris, Eileen Zanders, 117
Morris, Mitzi, 157

Morrison, Mr., 98
Moscardelli family, 163
Mothersingers Chorus, 83
Mountz, Homer, 127
Moyer, Martha, 128
Moyer, Warren, 98
Mundis, Carol, 128
Mundis, Jerry, 128
Mundis, Tom, 126
Murphy, George, 155
Myers, B., 86
Myers, Marlynn, 81
Myers, Mary, 40
Myers, Sandy, 81

N

Nance, Pam, 112
Natale, Al, 120
Natale, Frank, 120
Navy Club, 55
Neal, Charles, 85
Neal, Marlene, 85, 141
Neathery, Robert, 21
Neese, Mr. and Mrs. Tracy, 144
Nemecz, Charlie, 136
Nesch, Roger, 136
Neureither, Warren, 31
Nicetius, Brother, 31
Nichelson, Leo, 144
Nickelson, Dorothy, 144
Nika, Bob, 147
Nimmo, Niles, 126, 128
Nolan, Carl, 108
Nolan, John, 150
Nolan, Maxine, 83
Nonneman-Hiler, Judy, 80
Noonan, Audrey, 162
Noonan, Matt, et al., 162
Noonan True Value, 162
Nordain, Priscilla Mallory, 69
Norvel, William M., Jr., 95

O

O'Brian, Hugh, 108
O'Brien, Adelaide, 112
O'Brien, Florence, 112
O'Brien, Gene, 144
O'Brien, Mr. and Mrs. Robert, 144
O'Connor, Paul, 81
O'Connor, Bishop William, 81
O'Dell, John, 40
Oliver, Ann, 144
O'Neil, Bob, 81
Ori, Joe, 126, 128
Orlandini, James, 80
Orr, Beverly, 143
Ostermeier, Alfred, 128
Ostermeier, Bertha, 104
Ostermeier, Carl, 78, 98, 104, 108, 128, 154
Ostermeier, Carole, 78, 128
Ostermeier, Carole Jean, 126
Ostermeier, Caroline, 104
Ostermeier, David, 126
Ostermeier, Delmar, 104
Ostermeier, Ernest A., 116
Ostermeier, Fred, 104
Ostermeier, Robert, 104
Ostermeier, Ruth, 104
Ostermeier, Sue, 24, 78, 122, 126,

128
Ostermeier, William, 104
Ostermeier family, 35
Owens, Judy, 145
Owens, Lynn, 145
Owens, Mrs. Alfred, 145

P

Paige, Satchel, 34
Palmer, Tom, 81
Panther Creek Bowhunters, 137
Paoni, Dorothy, 34
Paoni, Fred, 34
Paoni, Kathleen "Babe," 34
parades, 24, 29, 64, 72
Paris, Tom F. "Cactus," 128
Parker, Morris, 112
Parnell, Peggy, 80
Pasowicz-Macleod, Irene, 80
Patey, Lorelei, 91
Patrick, G.W., 48
Patton, Joe, 86
Paulsel, Mr. and Mrs. Earl C., 112
Payne, Diane, 102
Payne, Harold, 102
Pearson, Emmet F., 112
Peontel, Nancy, 40
Perkins, Aileen, 97
Peterman, Mrs., 81
Peters, Betty, 21
Peters, Everett R., 33
Peters, Walter, 110
Peterson, Edith, 83
Petrella, Charleene, 80
Petschauer, Joyce, 40
Pettiford, John, 95
Pettit, Floyd, Jr., 95
Pfeiffer, T., 72
Philman, Ernest, 124
Philpott, Jay, 126
Pickett, Boyce W., 39
Pickett, Carl, 73
Pickett, Patricia Cook, 39
Pickett, Suzanne, 80
Pierce, Kay, 136
Pierce, Mark, 147
Pietzak, Ted, 81
Piiparinen, Barbara Snodgrass, 78
Pillsbury Co. employees, 66
Pitchford, David, 129
Pitchford, Pamela, 129
Plain, Nova, 83
Pleasant Grove Baptist Church, 145
Pleasant Hill School students, 40
Pleasant Nursery, Inc., 163
Plesch, Joe, 85
Pline, Richard, 112
Plohr, Bob, 81
Poole, Ed, 88
Poos, Omer, 153
Popjoy, Walter T., 31
Porter, Phyllis, 136
Porter, Richard, 73
Post, Donald, 72, 108
Powell, James Willis, 95
Powell, Paul, 46, 138–39
Power, Cathy, 136
Power, Niece, 50
Preckwinkle, George and Rosalee, 165
Proctor, Janet, 112

Provines, Bill, 73
Public Market employees, 74

Q

Quigley-Pickett, Suzanne, 80
Quinlan, Carolyn, 64
Quinnigan, Helen, 34

R

Race, Ken, 135
Radosevic-Gangitano, Theresa, 80
Ramelow, George, 50
Ramelow, Larry, 80
Randolph, Mary, 122
Raney, Mr. and Mrs. Stan, 82
Rapps, John, 80
Ray, S., 51
Reagan, S., 51
Rechner, Donna, 80
Reddick, Lillian, 139
Redpath, Don, 155
Reed, Mrs. Gerald, 144
Rees, Tyre, 96
Refine, Don, 113, 130
Renfro, John, 145
Renfro, Selma, 145
Rentsch, Dick, 126
Reynolds children, 30
Rhodes, Larry, 113
Rhodes, Rhonda, 101
Riba, John, 64
Richie, John, 73
Richter, David, 131
Richter, Max F., 79
Richter, Nancy, 120
Ridgeway, Ed, 126
Riechert, Gary, 122
Rieck, Harvey, 113
Riley, Gene, 21
Riley, Imogene, 21
Riseman, Ned, 104
Ritter, Betty Meiron, 45
Road Runners Hot Rod Club, 113, 130
Roberts, George C., 33
Roberts, Mary, 83
Robertson, Dick, 81
Robinson, Barbara, 73
Robinson, Dale, 21
Robinson, Emmett W., 95
Robinson, Floyce H., 95
Robinson, Frank, 34
Rock, Joseph, 80
Rock, Theresa, 50
Rodems, Jennie, 141
Rodger, Art, 112
Rodger, Jack, 112
Rodier, Louis, 33
Roesch, Walt, 153
Rogers, Clara, 80
Rogers, Elizabeth, 118
Rogers, Glen and Betty, 98
Rolle Bolle players, 57
Rollet, Joyce, 122
Ross, Edna, 145
Rowland, Bill, 81
Rowland, Julie, 141
Rudin, Carl, 10
Rush, Janet, 81
Russell, Jane, 72

Rutherford, Adrian, 112
Ruth Fortune Dancers, 69
Ryan, Danny, 108

S

Saccamano, Andy, 135
Sacred Heart School students, 50, 80
Sakris, Shirley, 21
Saladino-Eckhoff, Frances, 80
Sallenger, Barb, 128
Salzman, Karen, 91, 101, 136
Sando, Mary F., 83
Saner, Bob, 82
Sankey, John E., Sr., 33
Sapp, Leonard W., 161
Sargeant, Joann, 40
Sargent, A.L., 33
Schaad, Merle E., 31
Scheafer, Dale, 128
Schiefinger, Mary Ellen, 81
Schmitz, James R., 31
Schroeder, Barbara, 156
Schroeder, Keith, 108
Schull, Larry, 120
Schultz, Bill, 128
Schweighart, Sue, 126, 128
Scott, Dempsey, 95
Scott, Virginia, 36
Scott, William, 95
Seaborn, Bob, 77
Seaborn, Marlene, 157
Searcy, Mrs. Earle, 82
Seebach, Gloria, 91
Seiders, Rita, 80
Seitz-Parnell, Peggy, 80
Senor, Clarence, 34
Senor, Mr. and Mrs. Earl, 66
Senor, Mr. and Mrs. Walter, 66
Serapicon, Brother, 31
Settles, Don, 104
Sexton, Ronald, 80
Sharp, Lyle, 128
Shea, Joe, 155
Sheehan, Mr. and Mrs. James, 144
Shelton, H., 86
Shepard, C., 86
Shepard, Ivan, 144
Shephard-Eilers, Joan, 80
Sherman High School students, 113
Shipp, Corrine, 83
Shipp, Donald, 73
Shoemaker, Ken, 104
Shofner, Vivian, 93
Shomidie, Loretta, 19
Shomidie children, 22
Shoutz, Vernon, 156
Sieland, George, 13
Simmons, Justine, 145
Simpkins, Jesse, 95
Simpson, Bud, 144
Sims, Darlene, 118
Sims, Shirley Snodgrass, 67
Singleton, Marjorie, 95
Singleton, Rose, 95
Sink, Judy, 105
Skaggs, Nancy, 122, 128
Skating Regulars Club, 19
Skube, Louise, 107
Skube, Tom, 107, 135
Slagle, Enola, 83

Slaughter, Jerilee, 126, 128
Smith, Albert, 95
Smith, Bill, 98
Smith, Bob, 135
Smith, Carlena, 95
Smith, Donald, 21
Smith, Henry Dale, 104
Smith, Irv, 131, 150
Smith, J. Emil, 82
Smith, R., 86
Smith, Shirley, 74
Smith, T., 86
Snodgrass, Shirley, 67, 105
Snow, John, 80
softball teams, 34, 64
Sommers, Albert, 157
Sotak, Eddie, 112
Spence, Les, 120
Spencer, Charles, 131
Spencer, Randy "Big Boss," 150
Spencer, Ronald, 73
Spicer, Sharon, 126
Spindel, Russell, 21
Springer, Terry, 136
Springfield Ceramics and Crafts Club, 58, 93, 154
Springfield Fire Department, 11, 62, 86, 135, 157
  fires, 22, 30, 62, 94, 102, 156
Springfield High School students, 93, 136, 151
Springfield Municipal Band, 55, 127, 150
Springfield Optimist Club, 116
Springfield Police Department, 58
Springfield Sepian Club, 37
Springfield Symphony, 120, 154
Springfield Theatre Guild, 112
Springfield Transportation Company employees, 8
Springfield Urban League, 19
Springfield Women's Association of Golf, 141
Staab, Mr. and Mrs. James, 144
Staber, Robert, 80
Stadtman, Steve, 136
Stalets, Marilyn Zanders, 29
Stark, Dave, 128
The State Journal Register, 158
Stebbins, Susie, 126, 128
Steiger, Bill, 82
Steinkroger, Carl, 81
Stevens, Linda, 126
Stevenson, Adlai E., 31, 48, 49, 96
Stewart, Emma Lee, 69
Stieren, Ann, 144
Stites, J., 86
St. James Trade School students, 31
St. Joseph School students, 81
Stout, Paul, 98
Stratton, William G., 52–53, 78, 109
Strawn, Bubble, 157
Stritzel, Josephine, 144
Stroble, Helen, 39
Stroemer, Mark, 156
Stroemer, Steve, 156
Strongman, Vernon, 157
Stuart, Bill, 82
Stuckey, Gerald C., 151

Stuper, John, 45
Suarez, Silver, 157
Sullivan, G., 86
Sullivan, Norma, 21
Sullivan, Pat, 128
Summers, Dale, 126
Sunley, Grace, 91
Swan, Lynda, 136
Swango, Ann, 148
Sweet Adelines, 118
Sweisberger, Georgeene, 21
Swienfurth, Carl, 33
Swinford, Ted, 112
Sykes, George, 67
Syson, Velma, 126

T

Tallman, Mary Ellen, 101
Tate, Dick, 34
Tate, Gail, 81
Tatum, Joseph, 95
Taylor, Mildred, 73
Taylor, R., 73, 86
Taylor, Rose, 150
Teater, Jerry, 81
Teer, David, 50
Tepker, George, 136
Thomas, Donna, 81
Thomas, Lois, 95
Thomas, Mary Beth, 104
Thomas, Stan, 82
Thomas Rees Memorial Carillon, 129, 131
Thompson, Bertha, 83
Thompson, Donald, 95
Thompson, Floyd, 20
Thompson, Maenell, 156
Thompson, Mona, 104
Thompson, Mrs. Milton D., 110
Thortons, Mr. and Mrs. Joe, 66
Tibbs, Jacqueline, 83
Tillman, Dean, 86
Timms, Shirley, 73
Tinsley, Thomas, 95
Tisckos, Chuck, 136
Tomko-Tykal, Marcia, 80
Tomlin, Joe, 40
Tompkins, Floyd, 83
Tooker, Priscilla, 144
tornado damage, 102
Townsend, Dallas, 108
Townsend, Michael, 80
Townsend, Ruth, 83
Towsley, Donald, 27
Trede, Norma, 144
Troop, Harry, 112
Truax, W., 86
Truman, Harry, 46, 96, 138–39
Tucker, Linda, 136
Turner, Earlene, 73
Turner, Mr. and Mrs. Herman, 66
Tykal, Marcia, 80

U

Uchaez, Bertha Ostermeier, 104
Underwood, Carolyn, 81
Unique Matronettes Club, 36
Upton, Mary, 83
Urbanckas, Alfred, 110
U.S. Marine Band, 11, 42

V

Van Buskirk, M.G., 122
Vandegrift, William, 86, 94
Van De Wiele, William, 57
Van Doren, Mamie, 108
Van Hauwaert, Paul, 57
Vanselow, Linda, 128
Vernor, Frank R., 112
Verticchio, Paul, 153
Vetter, John, 155
Victor, Ida R., 141
Volk, B., 86
Volk, Vicki, 120
Volle, Bob, 129
Vose, Bob, 135
Vose, Jim, 50
Vost, Tom, 120
Vrona, Keith C., 112

W

Wagner, Marjorie M., 154
Wales, Valerie Edwards, 126
Wallace, Linda, 148
Wallace, R., 72
Walter, Lillian, 145
Wander, Al, 104
Wander, Mary, 104
Wander, Mary Beth, 104
Wander, Paula, 104
Warhurst, Jon, 108
Warless, Willa Jean, 139
Warren, Jackie, 135
Warren, Mickey, 82
Watkins, Jacqueline, 80
Watkins, Jim, 40
Watkins, Mary, 28
Watson, Jimmie, 34
Watson, Mrs. Jon, 156
Watt, Margaret, 91
Watt, Vicki, 136
Waughop, Mrs. Richard, 154
Weber, Anne, 120
Weber, Carl H. "Sagebrush," 128
Weber, David, 81
Weber, Janet, 148
Weber, Rex A. "Piute," 128
Webster, Dr., 59
Webster, George, 24
Webster, M., 86
Wells, Mark, 136
Welsh, Mary J., 83
Wendell, Don, 144
West, Harold Dean, 124
West, John, 124
West, Othel Brown, 69
West, Wayne, 124
West, William and Ella Mae, 124
Westminster Presbyterian Church, 44, 70, 81, 99, 105
White, Cecelia, 36
White, Dick, 112
White, James, 152
White, Jerry, 155
White, Jonette, 128
Whitthorne-Snow, John, 80
Wicks, Ed, 101
Wicks, Jack, 127
Wilborn, Linda, 128
Wilcoxson, Carol Sue, 72
Wilcoxson, Harry, 110

Wilcoxson, Jimmy, 110
Wilkinson, Norma, 143
Willey, Ron, 136
Williams, Barbara, 57
Williams, Ben, 147
Williams, Cathe, 136
Williams, H., 86
Williams, Joel, 95
Williams, Kevin, 147
Williams, Lynn, 136
Williams, Wayne F., 110
Willis, Jody, 81
Wilson, Bertha, 141
Wilson, David and Reva, 147
Wilson, Gerald, 73
Wilson, Gregory, 126
Wilson, John H., Jr., 45
Wilson, Laverne, 113
Wilson, Robert, 150
Wilson, S., 51
Wilson, Shirley, 91
Windsor, Al, 135
Wingerter, Bill "Pegwill Pete," 108
Wingerter, Will "Wild Bill," 128
Winstead, D., 51
Winstead, N., 51
Wolf, Jack, 73
Wood, Gary, 126
Wood, Joan, 105
Wood, John, 21
Woodcok, Karen, 122
Woodrum, Arlene Wilson, 85
Woods, Ellen, 40
Woods, Mary Jane, 40
Woods, Penny, 91
Woody, Pete, 126, 128
Woolery, Letha, 145
Woolridge, Sylvester, 95
Wright, Genevieve, 145

X

Xamis, Angeline, 83

Y

Yates, D., 86
YMCA "Big Bosses," 128
Yoggerst, Bill, 144
Yoggerst, Dave, 144
Yokem, Mary, 145
Young, Bea, 73
Young, Charles E., 152
Young, R.B., 128
Yung, Roy, 153

Z

Zanders, Elora, 92, 117
Zanders, Joseph, 29, 92, 123
Zanders, Marilyn, 29, 92, 117
Zaubi-Cummins, Nancy, 80
Zellman, George, 92
Ziegler, Edward, 99
Zillion, Dick, 126
Zimmerman, Judy, 93
Zink, Ellen, 80